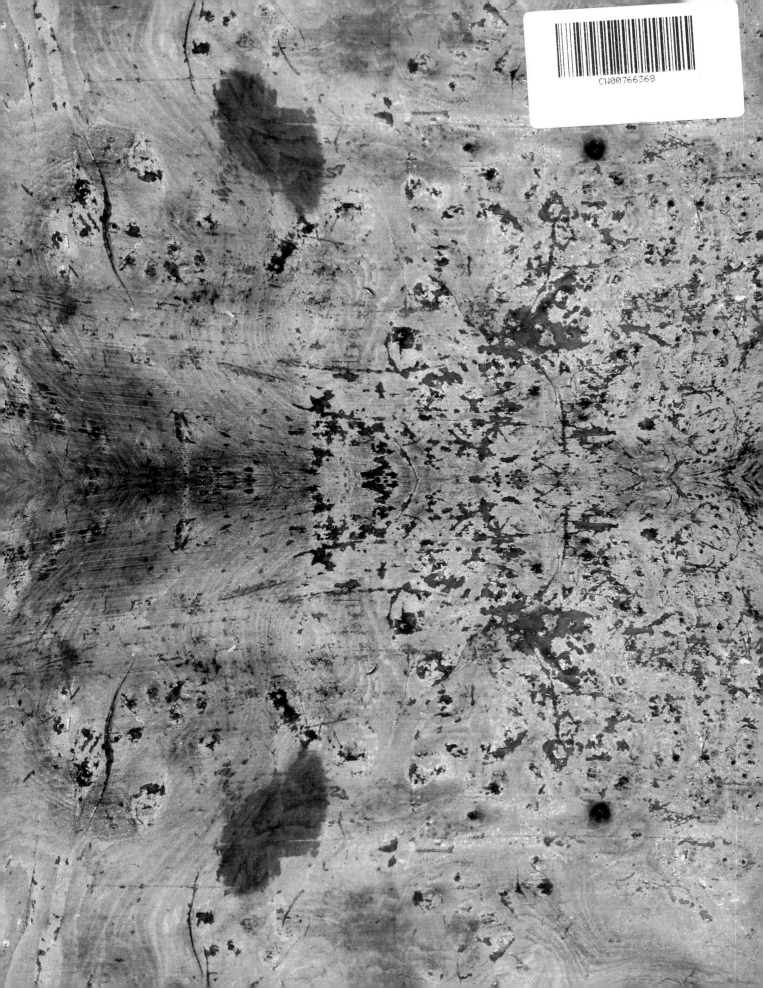

TREEN
for the Table

WOODEN OBJECTS
RELATING TO EATING AND DRINKING

Early engine-turned 'York' tankard, lignum vitae, made around the second quarter of the 17th century. See page 42.

TREEN
for the Table

WOODEN OBJECTS
RELATING TO EATING AND DRINKING

JONATHAN LEVI

IN CONSULTATION WITH
ROBERT YOUNG

Antique Collectors' Club

ISBN 1 85149 284 4

British Library Cataloguing-in-Publication Data
A catalogue record for this book is available from the British Library

Printed in England
by the Antique Collectors' Club Ltd., Woodbridge, Suffolk
on Consort Royal Satin paper
supplied by the Donside Paper Company, Aberdeen, Scotland

The Antique Collectors' Club

The Antique Collectors' Club was formed in 1966 and quickly grew to a five figure membership spread throughout the world. It publishes the only independently run monthly antiques magazine, *Antique Collecting*, which caters for those collectors who are interested in widening their knowledge of antiques, both by greater awareness of quality and by discussion of the factors which influence the price that is likely to be asked. The Antique Collectors' Club pioneered the provision of information on prices for collectors and the magazine still leads in the provision of detailed articles on a variety of subjects.

It was in response to the enormous demand for information on 'what to pay' that the price guide series was introduced in 1968 with the first edition of *The Price Guide to Antique Furniture* (completely revised 1978 and 1989), a book which broke new ground by illustrating the more common types of antique furniture, the sort that collectors could buy in shops and at auctions rather than the rare museum pieces which had previously been used (and still to a large extent are used) to make up the limited amount of illustrations in books published by commercial publishers. Many other price guides have followed, all copiously illustrated, and greatly appreciated by collectors for the valuable information they contain, quite apart from prices. The Price Guide Series heralded the publication of many standard works of reference on art and antiques. *The Dictionary of British Art* (now in six volumes), *The Pictorial Dictionary of British 19th Century Furniture Design, Oak Furniture* and *Early English Clocks* were followed by many deeply researched reference works such as *The Directory of Gold and Silversmiths,* providing new information. Many of these books are now accepted as the standard work of reference on their subject.

The Antique Collectors' Club has widened its list to include books on gardens and architecture. All the Club's publications are available through bookshops world wide and a full catalogue of all these titles is available free of charge from the addresses below.

Club membership, open to all collectors, costs little. Members receive free of charge *Antique Collecting*, the Club's magazine (published ten times a year), which contains well-illustrated articles dealing with the practical aspects of collecting not normally dealt with by magazines. Prices, features of value, investment potential, fakes and forgeries are all given prominence in the magazine.

Among other facilities available to members are private buying and selling facilities and the opportunity to meet other collectors at their local antique collectors' clubs. There are over eighty in Britain and more than a dozen overseas. Members may also buy the Club's publications at special pre-publication prices.

As its motto implies, the Club is an organisation designed to help collectors get the most out of their hobby: it is informal and friendly and gives enormous enjoyment to all concerned.

For Collectors — By Collectors — About Collecting

ANTIQUE COLLECTORS' CLUB
5 Church Street, Woodbridge, Suffolk IP12 1DS, UK
Tel: 01394 385501 Fax: 01394 384434
——————— or ———————
Market Street Industrial Park, Wappingers' Falls, NY 12590, USA
Tel: 914 297 0003 Fax: 914 297 0068

In memory of the joys of the chase for treen
with my wife Mary and son David
and dedicated to all you collectors and dealers out there
and the fun you are going to have in the future

Contents

Foreword

One day in 1988 the telephone in my office rang and a voice asked if it would be possible to look at our stock of treen. The owner of the voice arrived in due course and turned out to be Dr. Jonathan Levi who with his wife Mary spent some time looking over our collection and purchased a sycamore dairy bowl. I believe that it is true to say that neither Jonathan nor myself had the faintest idea that the purchase would lead to his passionate interest in wooden objects, the formation of a truly impressive collection, his son David taking up buying and selling treen as a career and, least of all, the authorship of this book, which is the first on the subject to be published in colour and the first major work on treen since *Domestic Utensils in Wood* by Owen Evan-Thomas, published in 1932, and the treen enthusiast's bible *Treen and other Wooden Bygones* by Edward Pinto, published in 1969.

This present work, which was intended to be more comprehensive, is now confined, due to ill-health, to wooden objects related to eating and drinking and it is in no way diminished by this. The knowledgeable, well-researched text and the excellent colour photographs bring to life the many facets of the subject and the chapters on the wooden utensils that graced the tables of our ancestors are augmented by a chapter on ornamental turnery by John Hawkins whose collection of rose engine turned objects contained the finest and most rare sixteenth and seventeenth century examples in the world.

The last four chapters are a graphic illustration of the inquiring mind behind this book. The author is well aware that the attribution of treen is not an exact science; the purpose of the object, the type of wood used and most particularly the age of the piece is very often down to sheer 'gut reaction' backed up by experience.

This book is a most welcome addition to the existing bibliography and will delight and inform all those interested in the fascinating world of treen.

Anthony Foster
January 1998

Preface and Acknowledgements

Ten years ago my wife and I discovered the world of treen and rapidly became avid collectors. In trying to educate ourselves and to learn more about the objects we admired, we rapidly ran into a brick wall. The main books on treen were written in 1932 (Owen Evan-Thomas), 1969 (Edward Pinto) and 1975 (Jane Toller). Though milestones for the collector, none had photographs in colour, all were out of print and rather out of date. In following our hobby we found the paucity of information and literature to be a major disadvantage, though in other ways it was also a challenge.

This book is written to share some of the fruits of our developing experience, the joys of the chase and the enlightenment that has come from tapping into the expertise of dealers and collectors, many of whom have become friends. But even more we are trying to provide some guidance to others through the relatively uncharted waters of treen collecting.

Our aim is to help inspire other collectors, many of whom may have started as ignorant as ourselves, to illustrate in colour examples of both commonplace and rarer pieces, to indicate where collections may be viewed, to provide a bibliography on what literature is available and to share our admiration of so many unknown craftsmen who configured everyday utilitarian objects into things of beauty and finesse. It is aimed to celebrate with extensive colour illustrations the richness of the feasting possibilities found in treen related to eating and drinking.

This is not intended to be the 'New Bible' on treen, nor to deal comprehensively with all turned wooden domestic objects. We have been particularly attracted by the objects related to eating and drinking, especially if they have a rich patination with appropriate signs of wear and usage. This has been widely interpreted to provide the main material for this book. The hope is that the colour illustrations will enthuse you with the joy of treen collecting.

My thanks are due to a more than dutiful wife who learned the joys of looking at treen rather than for china or jewellery at the antiques fairs we patronised and who came to share her husband's passion. My son has become particularly enthusiastic and his eagle eyes often spot treasures as he tours the country looking for stock – some of which has been known to enter our collection.

My particular and especial thanks are to Robert Young, expert *extraordinaire,* who has become a close friend. He has been more than generous in providing not only proper and very expert professional advice and guidance to an innocent beginner, but, more importantly, has been my very close consultant and adviser to ensure I didn't make too many glaring mistakes in my effrontery when writing this book on his subject. I am particularly grateful to him for the time, effort and enthusiasm that have been his crucial contributions.

John Hawkins over many years amassed a huge collection of seventeenth century rose engine turned treen, which caused a sensation when he brought it to the Olympia Antiques Fair in 1995. He has developed a particular expertise in this area and has been kind enough at very short notice to write this chapter and so share his knowledge and expertise not only with me but with other collectors. Axel Vervoordt bought the Hawkins Collection and has kindly allowed me to photograph some of his pieces for this publication.

Other treen collectors have been extraordinarily generous in allowing me to photograph some of the prizes in their collections for inclusion here and so greatly enhance the breadth of objects illustrated. These include Edward Harrison, Ian Turner, Tony Robinson, Ric Gijsen, CIS, JP., DL. and other anonymous private collectors. I am enormously indebted to them for their contribution to the enrichment of this book.

Early mazers very rarely come to the market. The renowned St John mazer was sold by Woolley & Wallis in 1997 and they have kindly allowed me to publish its photograph. Other photographs have been provided by Hampton Court Palace, the British Museum, the Victoria and Albert Museum, the Mary Rose Trust and the Wycombe Museum.

Quality photography is key to the attraction of this book. Unless otherwise indicated all the photography has been done by Andy Johnson and Joe Seaforth of Premier Photography Ltd. I am very grateful to them for the consistently high quality pictures they have produced within an extremely tight time schedule.

Tony Foster is a leading expert on treen and he has been kind enough to write a welcoming foreword to my efforts.

My plan had been to produce this book after my retirement from medical practice. Unfortunately I have fallen into medical hands and my plans have had to be expedited.

I have had to sacrifice the depth of research I had intended to do and to restrict severely the number of dealers and private collectors I have approached to lend objects. On the good side is the stimulus this book may have given to other enthusiasts to research some of the many fascinating areas of our ignorance and eventually burst into print and pictures for the greater good of us all.

In spite of the limitations of this book, I hope I have been able to transmit some of our enthusiasm for these old bits of wood to you, our readers.

Introduction

Who made Treen?

There is a romantic notion that items of treen were turned or whittled away by the local village carpenter or turner. Though for certain functional items such as platters or spoons this may have been true, it is now clear that workshops of varying size produced large numbers of similar objects. One only has to look at the pictures of chairs in the Chilterns being taken to market, or bodgers in the beech woods or local markets with piles of bowls and ladles for sale, to understand the scale of production of some items by particular workshops. This may account for the similarity of some pieces found. Earlier (pre-1800) pieces are now sufficiently uncommon to make it difficult to find similarities that correctly indicate specific workshops. Further, certain styles may have been regional so that one turner may have been influenced by the designs of a neighbouring competitor if his had been particularly successful.

Some pieces of treen have been turned with consummate skill, perhaps best exemplified by rose engine-turned wassail bowls and goblets, and these we know were not produced by the same individual who was making more mundane domestic objects.

Tradition and folklore surround Welsh love spoons. The common belief is that they were whittled away individually by a lover for a betrothed during the long winter evenings. Certainly some are so individualistic and unique in design and craftsmanship that this rings true. However, other designs, particularly some of the more complex examples with loose balls cut from the solid and left enclosed within the structure, have clearly been commercially produced. Multiple similar examples are available for comparison and study. Details of some examples are illustrated (see Plate 9/13) A review of love spoons in the National Museum of Wales' Collection clearly endorses this theory where several almost identical spoons are seen including five with chip-carved decoration and bearing the same date and initials, 'M+N 1836'.

The spoon left of centre in Plate 9/13, despite its complexity, is exceedingly close in design to the forks illustrated in Pinto (plate 161 C&D), the spoon in a Sotheby's auction in 1984 and another in Phillips auction (10.9.93, lot 486), as well as the National Museum of Wales spoons nos. 45, 46 and 47.

Similarly the 1849 fruitwood love spoon in Plate 9/13, right of centre, must have been made in the same workshop as others bearing different dates such as lot 678 from the Shepherd Collection sale, plate 57H in Evan-Thomas, another in the National Museum of Wales, no.1059 dated 1872, and plate 9 in *Welsh Folk Customs* by Trefor M. Owen.

With this evidence we must now accept that certainly by the second quarter of the nineteenth century there were some commercially produced love spoons. In contrast, there are only two out of the very large number of muffineers examined for this book that can be regarded as identical twins.

In conclusion, we have an overall picture showing a wide range of expertise and specialisation from the 'jobbing' village turner or 'bodger' through the skilled craftsman's workshop to the grand Gentleman or Court turner producing complex rose engine turning.

Pole Lathe Turning

Pole lathes are probably one of the most ancient tools developed by man. It is proven that turning dates back at least to 300BC and may have been introduced to England by the Iron Age Celtic people in around 200BC. Pole lathes were in continuous use in this country until the middle of the present century. For detailed discussions of pole lathes the reader is referred to the two articles in *Period Home* by Richard Filmer and to the chapter in *Folk Life* by J. Geraint Jenkins.

The pole lathe itself consists of a bed with two stocks of hardwood between which the wood to be turned could be fixed. Each has a spike for this fixing. The power comes from a long sapling, often of ash, between nine and twenty feet long. The thick end is securely fixed to the ground with the thin end directly over the bed. A cord or piece of leather is fixed to the top thin end, wound round the

Alexander Dean, a turner, at his pole lathe in the 1930s. Courtesy of the Ronald Goodearl Collection, Wycombe Museum

wood to be turned, and then fixed to a treadle on the floor, usually constructed in triangular form.

The principle is to fix the object between the centre spikes, rotate it by pressure on the treadle, with 'unwinding' reverse rotation following on release of that pressure, due to the springiness of the sapling producing a reciprocal and not a continuous rotary motion. The turner applies a sharpened chisel to the rotating object and with great skill produces his turned piece of treen, be it goblet, chair leg or whatever. The skill is in learning to co-ordinate hand and foot, releasing the pressure on the chisel during the 'rebound phase' when the object is rotating the wrong way, and to work the whole length of the object being turned. The inefficiency of this method is that the object, depending on its thickness, may only make about five revolutions with each down stroke on the treadle. The joy for us is the recognition of the irregularities in the turning and appreciation of the skill of the turner in producing such elegant objects with such primitive tools. A benefit of a contra-rotating pole lathe is that handles, such as on lamhogs, can be produced that would be impossible to make on a rotary lathe which operates with continuous revolutions.

Pole lathe turning inevitably leaves all the slight irregularities that characterise hand-made objects. The width, depth and fineness of the marks left by the chisel will be uneven compared with the perfection of the much higher speed mechanical rotary lathe. However, it would be a dangerous mistake to assume that broad irregular tooling can guarantee an early date. There are many factors to consider when attributing a date, as I hope to indicate in this volume. Primarily there is the density of the timber − close-grained hardwoods like lignum vitae, box or yew are likely to show less evidence of tooling than softer sycamore or fruitwood. Then there is the skill of the turner, the size and sharpness of his blades, and the length and flexibility of the sapling or spring and the length of his cord and thus the number of revolutions possible.

As collectors, of course, we cherish the traces left by skilful pole lathe turners, but can only use them for dating purposes in combination with stylistic considerations based on documented or dated examples in wood or other materials.

It is known that the pole lathe continued to be used long after the introduction of powered rotary lathes, which were much more efficient, because these were not available to the Chiltern bodgers who worked in the beech woods away from sources of power but close to an abundance of saplings. In the 1870s an incredible 5,000,000 chair legs were produced each year, such was the demand for chairs from the industry round High Wycombe. The bodgers had a flexibility with their pole lathes.

They didn't need to transport cumbersome timber, or keep a steam lathe fired up, and economically must have been competitive for many years.

Who used Treen?

It is worth remembering that the population of England was around 5.47 million in 1656, subsequently declined and only reached 5.9 million by 1751 and then rose rapidly to 8.7 million by 1801.

Some objects such as platters were used by all classes of society, until such time as more expensive and durable materials were adapted for use by wealthier households. Wooden platters are a good example. When introduced, probably in the Middle Ages, they were used universally until in the late seventeenth century platters began to be made in silver, pewter or ceramic. Initially these would only have been afforded by the nobility. Subsequently, as these materials became more commonplace, the wooden service, typically, was used by those in humbler dwellings. The use of other intricate or elaborate pieces such as wassail bowls, various goblets or other ornate drinking vessels may have been confined to the wealthier members of the community. Social and economic factors would determine the continued use of 'everyday' treen. Objects such as platters would not usually have been treasured possessions and when broken were likely to just be discarded or burnt.

The distribution of small bowls and platters found on the *Mary Rose* is particularly fascinating with the evidence suggesting that small bowls were the common drinking vessels and were individually owned while plates and dishes may have been communal.

What was made? What is it for?

Wood was the readily available and inexpensive material to make anything and everything an individual wanted or needed in the way of domestic utensils. Different woods have varied qualities of hardness, porosity, flexibility and taste which were known and understood, thus providing a range of qualities to suit particular functions. The size of tree was also a major determinant of a wood's use. Sycamore was a large tree, abundant, easy to turn, did not lend a taste and withstood washing up so these properties determined its use, making it particularly suitable for bowls, platters and spoons. In contrast yew and box were small trees providing close-grained hardwood to be used for different purposes. Wood was used as the basic material for making 'things', unless metal was crucial, as for instance in knives.

The interesting fact is that even though we now may have difficulty in discerning its function, every object was made for a specific purpose. The range of specialisation and specificity amazes as well as attracts us today. This may be particularly prominent with tools when one looks at the range of different spades for digging, or woodworking planes, each with its own specific and slightly different purpose. So when we are confronted by a carefully turned object now, whose purpose is not immediately obvious, it challenges our imagination to understand why our ancestor created it. Several examples are illustrated and discussed in Chapter 16.

Rarity and Popularity

The millionaires amongst you, dear readers, can aim at collecting seventeenth century armorial cups and covers, complete sets of Elizabethan roundels, methers, early rose engine turning, posset pots and the like. Mere mortals and wage slaves like us will have to be content to view these in museums and I have given some hints as to where good treen can be found in Appendix I. Many museums do not have their treen collections adequately displayed and should be encouraged to do so. The Pinto Collection in Birmingham is by far the largest and most comprehensive in Great Britain, yet only a small proportion of his pieces are out on view and these don't seem to be rotated with the reserve stock. Museum pressures seem to be such that even this premier collection is never introduced to a duster, let alone a sniff of beeswax.

Love spoons seem to have a special following and romantic appeal, so even relatively modest examples command a high price.

There are other areas such as egg cups, spice towers, oven peels, rolling pins (dough, oats and lace), platters, dairy bowls, dish slopes, quaiches, lemon squeezers, spoons, salts, muffineers or ladles which have not reached great heights of popularity and are still available at not astronomic cost. Each has potential special interest – limited time of production, social history, beauty, decorative possibilities, function, selection and employment of different woods, to name but a few. But even more important is the joy of the chase! Searching through markets, junk shops, antique centres, car boot sales, auctions and even one of the few remaining antique shops brings the anticipation of a find and an addition to your special area of interest. Added to that, on return home you have the benefit of the 'therapy' derived from polishing with lovely scented beeswax. The only reservation is that you must choose a wife with the same passion or you will find her looking at jewellery or even ceramics on your treen expeditions.

If you are a new collector visit a few museums (particularly the Pinto Collection in Birmingham) and specialist dealers and choose where your love lies and interest may develop. Try to concentrate on one particular area as specialisation offers the best hope for developing your own expertise as well as a fascinating collection.

Cleaning

You must ensure that you do not introduce woodworm into your collection and all pieces with worm holes that show any sign of activity whatsoever should be treated with one of the proprietary preparations which are highly effective, easy to use and, if left to dry out fully, do not stain the wood or spoil the patination. A syringe and needle may be particularly useful to ensure deep penetration of the killer liquid.

It is extremely rare for a treen object to need stripping. Very occasionally a piece may be found covered in modern paint. Even more rarely some old varnish may be so congealed with lumps and 'runny' marks, like those produced by a DIY amateur's over-enthusiastically applied paint, that stripping should be considered. If you have bought a piece in spite of these deficiencies, first consider discussing with your befriended dealer or restorer whether an expert should be asked to do the stripping or whether it is something you dare do yourself. Many more pieces have been seen that have been overcleaned or stripped than objects that might require stripping. Beware! Regrettably some dealers seem to think that a uniform brown stain enhances the appearance of their usually rather mediocre stock and so use it enthusiastically. This is difficult to remove without taking off any patina that might have been present. So ignore them and their stock unless they have maltreated an unrecognised treasure which then becomes your duty to rescue.

In this country treen is regarded as looking its best if waxed and polished. The advantages of this are that the wax helps to preserve the wood and its colour. Grain and patination are greatly enhanced. There are many preparations on the market and one with beeswax as the predominant ingredient should be chosen. If a piece is to be handled frequently a wax giving a harder surface may be desirable. To obtain this use a mixture with carnauba wax for a later coat. The highest polish obtained has been achieved with pure filtered beeswax in a little solvent though this surface readily shows finger marks.

If a piece hasn't been waxed for many years it may absorb a considerable amount so it can applied liberally in the first instance. Judge how dry it is by how quickly the waxed surface loses any stickiness. Later coats should be sparser and once an object has been fully treated it will only require rewaxing every four to six months. This need not stop you polishing more frequently without additional wax, an activity which improves the appearance of your collection and is therapeutic for you.

Varnishing

Organic oil and bone varnishing has been used for hundreds of years to protect wooden objects from liquids. Many pieces of treen were originally varnished and this should not be removed other than in extreme circumstances as already discussed. What is not widely realised is that though a varnish (or a wax) finish will protect against water in the liquid state it provides virtually no hindrance to the passage of water vapour. So no amount of waxing will prevent an object drying out, possibly excessively if exposed to central heating without humidification. Adequate humidification is essential for the happiness of your treen as well as all your other antique wooden furniture.

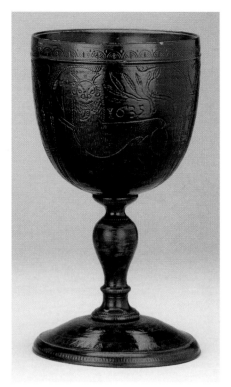

James I armorial cup from the British Museum dated 1635. This is apparently the only known dated example with a maker's name – ROBARTE ROVD
Courtesy of the British Museum

Dating

Most treen is not dated and it is even rarer for the maker to be known. The basis for dating must develop from the few known dated pieces and stylistic precedents in other materials. In a few areas, notably nutcrackers, sufficient examples are dated to establish a good factual background. A considerable number are illustrated here and they provide the basis for the dating of other pieces of similar style.

There are rather fewer known dated goblets so the examples available are particularly valuable. In most other groups dating is a prized rarity. There is a goblet in the British Museum of a pearwood standing cup of very similar style to several illustrated here dated 1635 but also inscribed 'MEAD BY ROBARTE ROVD'. Unfortunately nothing further is known about him. This group of cups is of uncertain origin and function and has provoked considerable interest and speculation without any real light being shed on the problems inspired. Investigation of this named maker could shed light on the mystery and a detailed study gathering together the known specimens in various collections and museums would make a fascinating project.

So, even if an object has an inscribed date, this must fit stylistically. One can't just indiscriminately believe dated objects. Beware!

All dating must be based on a knowledge of the development of style in similar objects made from other materials. Many wooden objects were made over decades if not hundreds of years without dramatic changes in style. There is no reason why a turner today could not produce a seventeenth century style goblet though he probably would not be using a pole lathe. So the rule is that an object cannot be any older than its most recent stylistic feature. Thereafter it must be a matter of judgement whether the surface, patination, colour and general wear and tear fit a particular age. A considerable knowledge is then required of the changing styles of objects in other materials such as silver as well as furniture. Even after considering all these factors there may be entirely valid differences of opinion. This should not upset a collector and will I hope not upset you, the reader, if you disagree with our best efforts to be helpful with dating. It is also why 'probably', 'about' and 'circa' are used liberally.

On making a purchase the aspiring collector should be given some understanding of the basis on which a putative date has been attributed.

In this book all measurements are in inches (to the nearest eighth). Unless otherwise indicated the height is given first followed by the diameter at the base.

Rare Welsh or border sycamore goblet with an interesting flat underside to the bowl, raised on a turned steeple stem on a circular foot. Interestingly the bowl shape is reminiscent of base metal mortars from the early part of the 17th century. It is branded with the initials SR to the inside and outside of the bowl. The underside has well defined and charming 'wobbly' tooling marks to the deeply concave foot. First quarter of the 17th century. 7in. x 4¼in.

CHAPTER 1

Wassail and Other Large Cups

Plate 1/1. A wassail bowl – see Plate 1/2 (3) – with an advertisement cut out from *The Times* in December 1997 thus showing that amongst 'top people' the word 'wassail' is not dead but still part of their daily language.

Wassail or lamb's wool bowls were characteristically made in the seventeenth and the early years of the eighteenth centuries. The name seems to have been derived from the Old English words 'Woes hal' meaning 'be whole' or 'be well'. The word 'wassailing' is associated with communal festive drinking, particularly on saints' days and holidays. The songs performed, the occasions and the recipes used have been quite extensively written about, particularly in the books by Edward Pinto (1949) and Owen Evan-Thomas (1932) and will not be repeated here. Essentially, a communal celebratory drink was made up, the ingredients being mixtures of ale or wine, heated with sugar, ginger, cloves, cardamoms, nutmegs, mace, cinnamon, apples and egg white which gave the frothy appearance and thus the name 'lamb's wool' bowls.

Wassail bowls were apparently first made when lignum vitae was imported into England from South America in the late sixteenth or early seventeenth century. The properties of this wood allowed the turner to give a bowl a greater depth than had been possible with English woods, such as maple, without causing splitting or subsequent leakage of the drink. It is thought that the previous generation of drinking vessels/mazers were often 'built-up' with silver rims in order to allow the vessel to have a greater depth and take a larger volume of liquid. Evan-Thomas suggests that the earliest (c.1620) wassail bowls were intermediate in depth between the mazers with deep silver rims and later wassail bowls. Speculatively this might be seen as a development as the turners of the day discovered that very large and deep bowls in lignum would not split or leak. Early wassail bowls had no light sapwood; the reason suggested is that the earliest logs of lignum imported were particularly large, allowing the turner to use just the heart wood.

No wassail bowls are dated. Pinto, from his experience, suggests that bowls with a depth 1in. to 3in. greater than the diameter were made in the first half of the seventeenth century and those with a steeply sloping foot are the

17

Plate 1/2. This selection of lignum vitae wassail bowls, all of the seventeenth century, are shown together to demonstrate something of the variety of shapes and sizes to be found. They all show the fine craquelure characteristically found in very old lignum.

1. Wassail bowl on a slightly knopped stem with a rose engine turned foot. A stem of this height is less common than the shorter ones seen in the other examples and may be a pointer to a date late in the 17th century. Good patination and wear. 12in. x 7½in. (bowl 6in. deep, 8in. diameter). **2.** Very unusual shape of wassail bowl with minimal foot and no stem. It has been suggested that these were designed for communal use – such as in an ale house – as they would be less likely to be knocked over. The colour is rich and the turning, particularly on the underside of the foot with its double concavity, is outstanding. Inside, the bowl has a petrified appearance while on the base

there is breaking up of the turning due to shrinkage, probably because it was used as a plant stand and kept wet. 17th century. 7¾in. x 7in. (bowl 6in. deep, 10½in. diameter). **3.** Very fine wassail bowl with outstanding colour and no damage. This bowl was sold by the dealer John Bly's grandmother for £5.10.0. on 30.9.40 to Mr. Trelawney Irving who was also charged 5s. for a copper liner to be made. It was sold back to John Bly in 1989. 17th century. 8¼in. x 7¼in. (bowl 5⅜in. deep and just over 7½in. diameter). **4.** Wassail bowl and cover with gilded acorn finial, a short knopped stem and with the interior painted with cream gesso. Previously in the Shepherd Collection (label no.01804) and sold at the Sotheby's sale lot 566. 17th century. 12in. x 6⅜in. (bowl 6½in deep and just over 7¼in. in diameter). **5.** Wassail bowl of smaller size with rather engaging distortion of the rim without any cracking. 17th century. 7¼in. x 5½in. (bowl 5½in. deep and 5¾-6⅛in. in diameter depending where it is measured).

The undersurface of the lid, magnificent in its simplicity, with the remarkable preservation of the undamaged and incorporated nutmeg grater.

Detail showing the complexity and depth of the rose engine turning and the nutmeg container and finial.

Plate 1/3. A rare and magnificent early 17th century English lignum vitae rose engine turned and faceted wassail bowl with a large finial nutmeg holder above the lid with its very rarely surviving nutmeg grater incorporated. The bowl is ten sided with a knopped stem and base, both of which are elaborately engine turned. 13¼in. x 6in.

Plate 1/4. Splendid wassail bowl in lignum vitae, previously in the Evan-Thomas Collection and illustrated in his book (plate 11). The strap-work reaching to the top of the bowl may be an early feature. Short simple concave stem. 6¾in. deep. 17th century. 10½in. x 8½in.

Plate 1/5. A 17th century English wassail bowl with lid and acorn finial. The body has three very thin bands of decoration above a short plain stem with a minimally stepped foot. 8¼in. x 5½in.

earliest. Post-Restoration (1660), the depth and diameter were about equal while later till the end of the century the diameter tended to increase while the depth decreased. Pinto's suggestion has not had general support from collectors or dealers. Occasionally the bowls had a long stem and very rarely no stem or a minimal foot. It is not clear whether these style differences were of regional or temporal significance. It would be an interesting exercise to document the variation in length, shape and decoration of the stems in a large group of bowls to try to clarify this further.

Many wassail bowl have some strap-work. The position, complexity and number of straps may again have some significance in relation to date. Earlier large drinking vessels made from coconuts or the shells of ostriches or other large birds needed strap-work to attach them to a stem for conversion into a drinking vessel. The strap-work on wassail bowls could be the stylistic vestigial memory of such designs.

Wassail bowls and dipper cups with deep rose engine turning are thought to be amongst the earliest. See Chapter 2 for more details.

Owen Evan-Thomas was a major collector and dealer in the 1920s and '30s. He writes that over one hundred wassail bowls had passed through his hands and that he had never found two with the same mouldings. He had major exhibitions of his drinking vessels in 1921 and 1939 as well as publishing his book in 1932. Some of his particularly important pieces can be seen in the Victoria and Albert Museum and the Burrell Collection in Glasgow.

Dipper cups in lignum, sometimes with silver strengthening bands round their rims, are closely associated with wassail bowls and, as illustrated, may have sophisticated engine turning. It is often said that they were placed on the multiple tall finials found on the lids of some of the more elaborate wassail bowls. This seems unlikely as anyone who has put a dipper cup upside down on to a finial immediately sees how uncomfortable this feels and how unbalanced the cup is. No specific function for the finials other than decoration has been proposed. I feel they must have had a specific function beyond this though we do not now have the knowledge or wit to discern it.

Plate 1/6. 9. An English lignum vitae wassail bowl with a short stem and two prominent bands decorating the centre of the deep bowl. 9¼in. x 7½in.

Plate 1/7. A small possibly late 17th century English lignum vitae wassail bowl of 'brandy balloon' outline with turned decoration to the bowl with the foot showing a small dome between two steps. 7¾in. x 6in.

Plate 1/8. A large lignum vitae late 17th century wassail bowl with a dipper cup in similar style. The bowl is unusual in having no stem or foot and has only a single simple rib to form a collar. See Pinto plate 34 for another without a foot. Bowl 9in. x 3¼in., dipper cup 2½in. x 2in.

Plate 1/9. Large richly grained lignum vitae English wassail bowl of late 17th century origin and without any decoration to the wide bowl which has 'punch bowl' proportions above a short wide stem and foot. 8in. x 6in.

Plate 1/10. 1. Exceptional rose engine turned lignum vitae wassail bowl cover, with remarkable deep turning around the finial. May date from c.1600. 7¼in. diameter. The underside (left) is also beautifully turned. The tragedy is that this has become separated from its bowl. Far left is a close-up to show the depth and complexity of the rose engine turning.

Plate 1/11. Four English silver-rimmed dipper cups all in lignum vitae from the 17th century.

1. A comparatively sturdy example with deeply turned decoration and a typical early 17th century scalloped and chased silver rim. 3in. x 1½in. **2.** A similar example, although more finely turned, with engine turning to the base and a silver rim with scalloped decoration. 3in. x 1¾in. **3.** A plain example with an attractive scalloped edge to the silver rim. 2⅝in. x 1¼in. **4.** An unusually small dipper cup with a very pretty engine turned base and a plain silver rim. 1½in. x 1½in.

Plate 1/12 (Above). 1 and 3. Pair of English rose engine turned lignum vitae dipper cups. First half 17th century. 2½in. x 1½in. **2.** English lignum vitae dipper cup surmounted by a silver rim with a scalloped edge below a reeded band. 17th century. 2½in. x 1¼in.

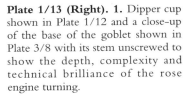

Plate 1/13 (Right). 1. Dipper cup shown in Plate 1/12 and a close-up of the base of the goblet shown in Plate 3/8 with its stem unscrewed to show the depth, complexity and technical brilliance of the rose engine turning.

Plate 1/14. A rare surviving pair of English lignum vitae dipper cups of similar size and identical decoration. Late 17th century. 2¾in. x 1¼in.

Plate 1/15. A pair of walnut wassail bowls also of late date that could well be intentional forgeries. Whilst they have an acceptable colour and semblance of patination they lack the depth and sincerity of genuine examples. Owen Evan-Thomas, having wide experience of handling and viewing period wassail bowls, states he only ever found them in lignum vitae and never discovered a pair.

This pair with the deeply incised ring turning discussed with the cup in Plate 1/16 shows no evidence of turning or chuck marks to the base; the slightly 'open and immature' grain and rather intentional looking distressing are sadly not the exception that proves the rule and must be considered 'dodgy'. They are of high educational value. 7¼in. x 6in.

Plate 1/16. This and the previous pair of walnut wassail bowls are considered to be 'wrong' and intentional forgeries, rather than just being imitations of an earlier style. Whilst this example has a generous flared foot and ball knopped stem below a beautifully proportioned bowl, all in keeping with a late 17th or early 18th century style, there are certain other factors to be considered in assessing its credibility. Firstly the deeply incised ring decoration to the outside of the foot, which this piece has in common with the pair of wassail bowls (Plate 1/15), is a feature we have not found on any other bowls of 'this date'; the everted raised lip moulding has no precedent and the underside of the foot has no definitive traces of turning. Superficially this example has an appealing fruity colour and a surface patination, but closer examination reveals no genuine surface or blistering or liquid staining to the bowl, and a rather too regular pattern of bruising and distressing. Finally there is no evidence of genuine wear to the undersurface of the foot. When we find an object with several stylistic anomalies and question its authenticity it is generally safer to assume the worst rather than to extol its virtues in its defence. It is still difficult to be dogmatic about the actual age of an item that all the 'rules' indicate is out of period. An attractive example such as this with no exact precedent might have been made at any time over the past hundred years or so. Just decipherable on the bottom is written 'Found in Oxford 1886 Burr maple loving cup'. There is also further, unreadable, writing. Hopefully other similar examples may appear to clarify this problem and establish a possible date and provenance. 8¼in. x 10in. at the rim.

Plate 1/17. English posset bowl of a particularly large size shown for comparison with a much smaller but unvarnished posset cup. The similarity of the design in the two sizes is striking. They both are made of plane tree wood and date from around the first quarter of the 17th century. The large one was reputed to have come from the Turner Collection. It has been covered many years ago in varnish giving it a rather uniformly dark surface. It has been turned significantly more thickly, possibly because of its larger size, but still has only one small crack. The smaller one is unvarnished, is in perfect condition, very thinly turned, without a crack or blemish, and has wonderful variation in colour. The foot is equally thinly turned with a deep concavity and screws on to the bowl. It is a remarkable survivor in a wonderful state. Interestingly, its extreme rarity allowed it to be largely unrecognised except by a few cognoscenti (and my son) at an auction at a major London house.

Plate 1/18 (Opposite). Large English walnut loving cup or chalice with knopped stem and very fine domed foot which looks characteristically English, and which dates it to about 1670. The wood appears to be French walnut. The nature and the position of the bands is probably derived from silver design where it originated as strap-work to hold large eggs or coconuts in early drinking vessels. 14in. x 6in.

CHAPTER 2

English Rose Engine Turning on Wood and Ivory in the Sixteenth and Seventeenth Centuries
by John Hawkins

The art of ornamental turning seems to have originated in South Germany centred around Augsburg in the first half of the sixteenth century, the medium for its execution being African elephant ivory. A good overview of sixteenth and seventeenth century European turning on the rose engine lathe is encapsulated in the book *Sovereigns as Turners*, Maurice, 1985, proving the origin of this type of work to be the prescribed occupation of the very rich, the cost of the lathe being the prime consideration.

From the late sixteenth century it was normal in German states to include an ivory turner at court. The Elector Augustus of Saxony (1533-86) and his professional assistant turned between them over 2,000 pieces. The collections of the Emperor Rudolph II (ruled 1576-1612) in Prague, the Archduke Ferdinand (1526-95) at Schloss Ambras, the Kunstkammers of Duke Albrecht V of Bavaria (1528-79) and the Elector William IV (ruled 1567-92) at Kassel all contained turned ivory. The ornamental turned ware collected by the Grand Dukes of

Plate 2/1 (Opposite). Monumental English ornamentally turned cup and cover with a 17th century silver rim strengthener. The stand may be the lid of an even larger wassail bowl of which this is the cup. It is similarly extravagantly turned on a rose engine lathe. c.1575. (Previously in the Evan-Thomas Collection.) The finial unscrews and underneath is a concealed chamber beneath the base for ground nutmeg with which to

flavour the drink. Its size and magnificence raise the possibility it was royal. I consider it to be one of the finest surviving mechanically made objects from Tudor England.

Plate 2/1A (Above). The lid of the cup opposite to show the technical mastery of this turner in being able to produce a finial and lid to the nutmeg grinder as such a *tour de force*.

A. Ivory rose turned case and the miniature of Ann of Cleves by Holbein. *Courtesy the Victoria and Albert Museum Picture Library*

Tuscany is still preserved in the Museo d'egli Argenti in Florence and the two volume catalogue of the Danish Royal Collection of curiosities illustrates nine boxes, the property of King Frederick III. In the 1560s his father, Frederick II (ruled 1559-88), had installed a Wunderkammer at Krogen under the supervision of his royal turner, centred on the lathe room in the castle.

Henry VIII was not to be outdone. Very much the modern sovereign of the sixteenth century, he attracted many clever Europeans to his Court, not the least the engineer Nicolaus Kratzer, the King's astronomer and instrument maker, who was in the Royal household by 1519. Kratzer is well known from his portrait surrounded by his instruments which was painted in 1528 by Hans Holbein (d.1543), court painter to Henry VIII. (There is a copy of this in the National Gallery, London, and the original is now in the Louvre.) Kratzer, Holbein and the Armourer to the Court, Holzmann, were all natives of Augsburg and maintained workshops and a studio adjoining the Royal Palace at Greenwich.

The first documented rose engine turned item of English work is the case of the miniature of Anne of Cleves (A). It is my opinion that this miniature case was inspired by contemporary European work. It is a sophisticated pun on the rose emblem or badge of the House of Tudor. It is well known that Holbein was sent

to Saxony in 1539 to paint the miniatures of Anne and her sister Amelia and that Henry agreed to the marriage based on Holbein's depiction of his future bride.

It has been impossible to determine the name of the turner capable of executing this complex work at the Tudor Court. The art of this unknown turner requires the use of an ornamental turning lathe fitted with a rose engine and the inherent skill to execute the complex patterns made possible by such a machine. The surviving eighteen English sixteenth century miniature cases and boxes known to the writer using this technique are all in ivory.

In 1720 George Vertue described the Anne of Cleves miniature as being 'in a round ivory box turned finely like a Rose with loose leaves'. Some fifteen Tudor miniature frames survive of varying degrees of complexity, the finest collection of which is in the Miniature Room of the Victoria and Albert Museum. They contain miniatures by Holbein (Anne of Cleves), Hilliard (1547-1619), Teerling (d.1576) and Isaac Oliver (d.1617). It is interesting to note that by 1625 either the fashion had changed or the skill had been lost, possibly as the result of the death of the turner, for no miniature cases of similar form after that date are known to exist.

Only two items which are not miniature cases seem to have survived from this time. One is the Parker Box on view in the Victoria and Albert Museum. Archbishop

Plate 2/2. The second similar cup with a replaced finial and without the later silver strengthener, probably made by the same master turner. c.1575. A rather similar example, though not so deeply turned, can be seen in the reserve collection at the British Museum – this is of particular interest in having a 17th century silver rim and a late silver boss inscribed 'OBS NEWARK 1646'.

Plate 2/2A. The underside of the lid to show the complexity of the rose engine turning.

Parker was head of the newly formed Protestant Church of England between 1559 and 1575 and he gave the box, with its companion jewel depicting Venus and Cupid at the Forge of Vulcan, to Queen Elizabeth, daughter of Henry VIII and Anne Boleyn, as evidenced by the documentation contained therein. Parker was previously chaplain to them both. Anne Boleyn was beheaded by

B. This ornamentally turned ivory jewel box is of similar form to that in the collection of the Victoria and Albert Museum and in the Danish Royal Kunstkammer. The rose badge of the Tudors is common to them all. The cutting of the petals is a test of skill mastered only by this unknown turner at the Tudor Court. English. c.1550.

C. (Below left) The standard of execution of the petals to this rose, although fine, is not in the same league as the jewel boxes. This may be interpreted as either a lack of skill or as a simple example of turning for a less demanding client. My interpretation is a lack of skill in the use of this complex equipment by a second generation operator. English. c.1610.

D (Below right). An ivory pomander. English, c.1560, by the turner to the Court of Henry VIII.

Henry in 1536 and I suggest that this jewel and its case was made for Anne and designed by Holbein who was by trade a jeweller. The box may well have been given by Anne to her chaplain at her execution to be held in trust for her daughter, Parker later, when Archbishop of Canterbury, returning it to her Protestant daughter Elizabeth. Illustrated is an almost identical Tudor jewel box from the John Hawkins Collection (B), an example of slightly less fine turning by his successor using the same lathe (C) and a pomander c.1560 (D).

A visit to the Victoria and Albert Museum will enable a comparison to be made between these ivory miniature cases and the wassail bowl on the table in the so-called Ashbourne Suite of two candlestands and candlesticks, a table, a wassail bowl and dipper cups. The unknown turner at the Tudor Court, using the same complex lathe, was unable to maintain this high standard of execution. By 1625 ivory had been replaced as a medium by lignum vitae, but the standard of execution, presumably using the same expensive royal lathe, seems to have diminished.

During the reign of Charles I and Cromwell's Commonwealth this workshop appears to have concentrated on ornamentally turned lignum vitae drinking vessels. Ivory is a constant — the turner knows what to expect and faults are rarely encountered when using this material. The same cannot be said for wood, which has to be well seasoned, tight grained and immensely hard to allow for the execution of such fine work. The timber used was exclusively lignum vitae. The precise date of its introduction into Europe is unknown, but, like tobacco, a date in the 1560s seems probable All sixteenth and early seventeenth century lignum vitae

Plate 2/3. Three English lignum vitae tankards. They appear to be turned by the same hand and stylistically date from c.1650. The form is based on London made silver tankards of this date which was fairly standard at that time. The one with the thumb-piece of divided horns is possibly the earliest, c.1640 and never had a lip. 6¾in. high. The one with the lip and an undivided thumbpiece may be c.1650 (5in. high) while the contemporary silver coat of arms on the largest gives a date no later than 1652. The silver rim is later and the thumbpiece is missing. 8¾in. x 6¾in.

vessels were turned from magnificent pieces of timber with no sapwood – the colour of bronze. Such a choice was presumably no longer available by the 1680s.

Neither the second or possibly third generation turner using the royal machine was able to extract its potential and we see a decline in terms of complexity of execution, much as today there are very few people, if any, that can extract the full potential from a Holtzapffel ornamental turning lathe. The Ashbourne lignum wassail bowl in the Victoria and Albert Museum is c.1620. The dipper cups, table, candlesticks and stands are c.1670. It is interesting that the history within the family of Lord Cullen of Ashbourne was that the suite was a gift from Charles I, after the Battle of Naseby, but while this could apply to the wassail bowl and is probably correct, the balance of the set is after 1660.

Rose engine turned cups
My collection contained two rose engine turned lidded cups, probably made by the same hand using the same lathe that produced the Anne of Cleves miniature case and the Archbishop Parker box. The pun on the Tudor rose, now executed in wood, is an incredible technical achievement, and says a lot for the strength and density of lignum vitae. The large cup on a stand dismantles, the finial unscrewing to reveal a secret chamber for the nutmeg, contained within the lid. The later silver rim is a mid-seventeenth century strengthener. The stand by the same turner to take the dipper cups may have come from an even larger wassail bowl. It is my opinion that this is one of the finest surviving mechanically made objects in wood of the Elizabethan age and I date it c.1575. A similar cup is illustrated; the finial, however, is later.

Tankards
It is possible to date surviving lignum tankards by comparing the decoration with that found on hallmarked silver examples.

An Elizabethan silver tankard bearing London hallmarks for 1597 has a simple barrel shape with reeded decoration (sold Christie's 15.10.85, lot 1233). Reeded decoration has often been considered mid-seventeenth century in its usage, but this tankard refutes that assumption.

The three tankards formerly in my collection can be dated from silver examples by their lid shape and thumb-

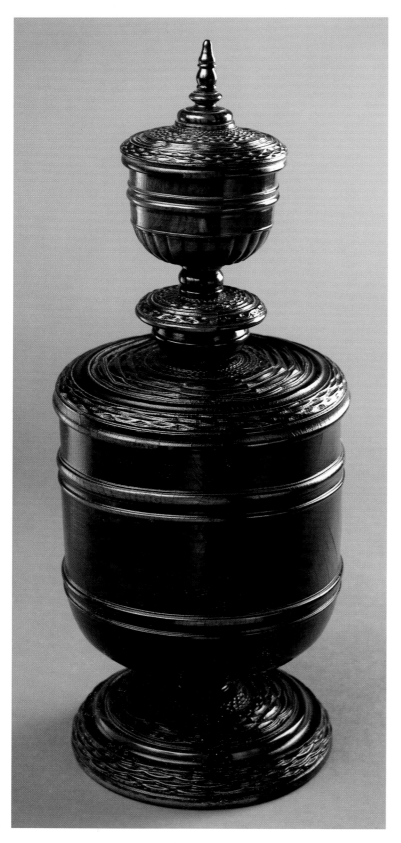

piece design. A tankard with a reeded body and thumbpiece with no horns but of straight-sided shape is known bearing the arms of the Archbishop of York for the year 1626 (Asprey advertisement, *Apollo,* July 1990). The earliest with a pointed front to the lid is 1638, sold to Lord Rothermere (Christie's 3.12.41, lot 63). The horn to the handle, however, is not divided. The earliest tankard with a divided horn to the thumbpiece, with straight sides and a pointed lid, is 1638. The earliest silver hallmarked London with a fully divided horn thumbpiece, pointed lip to the lid and handle of similar form to that shown in my wooden ornamentally turned tankards, in lignum vitae, is hallmarked for 1641 (exhibited Christie's 1955, exhibit 107).

These three lignum tankards are all by the same hand and from the above comments stylistically date between 1645 and 1655. Their design is based upon London silver tankards, which by then had reached this standard format.

Wassail bowls

The silver equivalent of a wassail bowl does not seem to exist and I think it would be safe to assume that all large communal drinking bowls, prior to the advent of the monteith, were made from lignum vitae. The earliest recorded silver monteith is for 1684 – three examples are known to survive. I suggest that in fact, rather than co-existing, they completely replaced the turned lignum wassail bowl, from 1685. Three of my wassail bowls are illustrated.

Plate 2/4. An English lignum vitae wassail bowl incorporating a loving cup for distribution of drink. The free standing cup unscrews from the nutmeg holder. c.1640.

Plate 2/5 (Opposite). A fine English lignum vitae wassail bowl with stands, possibly for dipper cups, and holes in the lid for clay pipes. In my opinion this was made by the inheritor of the machinery and equipment of the unknown Tudor turner c.1600. The concept of the rose turning is still present but without the depth and detailed skill of execution. It bears many similarities to the Ashbourne Suite wassail bowl and is in all probability by the same hand.

Plate 2/6A.

All the pictures illustrating this chapter (except the case and miniature of Ann of Cleves) are from the magnificent collection built up by John Hawkins over twenty years.

Plate 2/6 (Opposite). My favourite object in the collection. It has never gone out of shape so the wood must have been seasoned for many years. It is decorated all over and has a wonderful colour. The finial is a nutmeg holder which unscrews to reveal the grinder beneath. c.1620.

CHAPTER 3

Goblets, Mazers and Other Drinking Vessels

Plate 3/1. A rare small English burr maple 'monks' mazer bowl having an unmarked plain silver rim. The boss/print is now lacking but there is a trace left of the original fixing pin. It also sports an interesting silver wire repair to a small split on one side (see Plate 17/6). 16th century or earlier. 1½in. x 4¼in. at the rim.

This is a broad based chapter as it looks at mazers and other early drinking bowls along with a multifarious collection of drinking vessels and goblets that are not covered within the specific chapters on wassail bowls, or other vessels known to have originated in Scotland or Ireland.

The tightly grained and usually well figured burr of maple has been highly prized throughout Northern Europe since the Middle Ages. Apart from its natural beauty, the properties of burr maple lend themselves perfectly to serve as drinking vessels – namely, a lack of porosity and only minimal tendency to splitting. However, by their nature, the burr growths of maple trees are relatively small and the bowls turned from them reflect this limitation.

Important ceremonial and monastic mazers resplendent with raised precious metal rims to increase capacity, central bosses/prints and occasionally strapwork, often with chased decoration including coats of arms, stylised floral decoration and mottoes, are well documented.

There is a wealth of literature on mazers of this type (see Appendices IV and V) describing their form, provenance and details of their mounts. They are largely to be found in Museums, Oxbridge Colleges and major collections. Rather than reiterate previously published details of these aforementioned documentary pieces, I have chosen to illustrate four examples of previously unpublished mazers and burr maple vessels showing a variety of shapes and sizes, reflecting their original purposes. It should be noted here that whilst technically a mazer is described as 'a hardwood drinking bowl, usually silver mounted' there is an old school of thought that to be accurately described as a mazer the bowl should sport a silver boss/print in the middle of the bowl. However the origin of the word mazer in Middle English from old French 'masere' derived from Germanic is known to describe the maple timber itself and it is this that is important to the treen enthusiasts.

Even simple examples rarely appear on the open market and they are eagerly contested. However, wishful mazer

Plate 3/2. A rare burr maple and silver mounted loving cup or 'mazer bowl' of magnificent proportions. Unusually, the generous bowl is raised on a turned stem and flaring foot and the extraordinarily fine turning tapering up to such a thin rim suggests the work of a master turner. This was exhibited to the Royal Society of Antiquaries by the Rev. Danvers Grossman in 1892 who suggested it was Elizabethan or possibly James I. See the cover of Evan-Thomas' book (Appendix I) for a vessel of similar shape dated 1610. 6in. x 4¼in.

owners must beware because silver and white metal mounted rice and/or drinking bowls from India, Nepal, Afghanistan and the Far East can bear a vague passing similarity to the early English mazers. A strongly everted slightly 'roll-over' rim and a pronounced raised disc-shaped foot, sometimes clad in embossed silver, are features I have noted on foreign bowls I have handled. Unfortunately I have only a rather poor quality photograph of the example I was able to find for this book. Compare this with Plate 3/1 which illustrates the rare simple early mazer of English origin with which they could possibly be confused.

In relation to mazers and the tradition of drinking from

Plate 3/3. The St.John Mazer. This remarkable and well-documented mazer was sold at the Woolley and Wallis auction on 24.9.97, lot 386. The provenance was from Dr. Stukeley to the Rev. H.F. St.John to F.H.Cook and then by descent. The silver is hallmarked for London 1585 with the maker's mark – a caltrap. The print shows the arms of Cotes. The wood is burr maple and the handles are thought to be additions.

Courtesy Woolley and Wallis and David Robson Photography

bowls it is particularly interesting to note the result of the study of the wreck of the *Mary Rose* which is known to have sunk in 1545. No goblets and few tankards were found. Small bowls of various shapes and forms were found scattered around the ship, often scratch carved with initials and 'graffiti', unlike the platters which were discovered in large groups, many near the galley, as discussed by Alex Hildred in chapter 4 of the recently published *Artefacts from Wrecks*.

The conclusion drawn from this evidence is that each sailor had his own drinking bowl or bowls which he kept with him for personal use throughout the day and took along to meals, and that drinking from small wooden bowls of 'mazer' type was still prevalent amongst these sailors in mid-sixteenth century domestic and marine life.

Before the discovery and employment of lignum vitae as a popular material for drinking vessels in England, standing cups, goblets and chalices were common to the fashionable courts and wealthy Catholic churches of Renaissance Europe. There are many documented examples in public and private collections and shown in still life paintings in a multitude of materials. Gold, silver gilt, silver, enamel and glass were common materials employed, but there are also known examples of exotic shells, *coco de mer,* ostrich eggs, tortoiseshell, coconut, turned ivory and exotic timbers, all mounted on elaborate precious metal stems and feet true to the fashion of the

Plate 3/4A.

Plate 3/4 (Opposite). A rare early 17th century English maple wood loving cup of footed mazer form with single incised ring-turned decoration at the base and a simple flaring foot. The surface shows crusty degradation of varnish and deep build-up of genuine patina. First quarter 17th century. 5¼in. x 5⅛in.

Plate 3/5. Two English lignum vitae so-called 'York tankards' (I have been unable to substantiate a reason for this name) made around the second quarter of the 17th century.

Right. This early engine turned piece has similar turning on the body to several other known pieces. There is stylised rosette decoration on the lid, with a finial that appears original. The thumbpiece is missing, but the handle is original. Similar tankards are illustrated in the Shepherd Collection sale at Sotheby's (30.11.83 catalogue, lot no. 561), the article by Barbara Pearce and three tankards shown by John Hawkins at Olympia in 1995. This example is particularly well patinated and

elegant. Compare with the other one illustrated here and the ones in Plate 3/6 and Plate 2/3. With finial 5in. x 4½in.
Left. This has a non-hallmarked decorated silver band around the top and lid, with rosehead screws attaching the thumbpiece – all stylistically of a similar date to the previous tankard, c.1630-50. There is also a silver lining, hallmarked 1812, with a residual line where it was joined to the original silver band. There is evidence of some repairs to the handle which involved cutting away small parts of the silver rim and a little displacement of the lid. This is a fine example, but somehow not as elegant and without the fine patination of the slightly smaller tankard. 5½in. x 5in.

High Renaissance and mannerist style from 1450-1600.

It is these high footed, sometimes lidded goblets that can be traced as the stylistic precedent for late sixteenth and early seventeenth century goblets and steeple cups. Taste and fashion in seventeenth century England was dictated by the wealthy courts of the Continent and introduced here by Huguenots and other European craftsman. With the introduction of lignum vitae towards the beginning of the seventeenth century a new and exotic material, impervious to the effects of liquids, was available to be fashioned into drinking vessels and a specifically English style of treen began to develop from around the middle of

the century. Largely we remain ignorant of everyday domestic wooden vessels prior to 1650 but we can suppose, backed by evidence from the *Mary Rose,* that the simple drinking bowl may have persisted longer than previously reckoned in modest homes and taverns.

There is a huge range of different wooden cups and goblets made between 1580 and 1900 and I have selected a wide variety to illustrate the variations in type and development in styles from 1600-1850, from the museum quality pieces through to humble domestic examples that may be found at the local market or antiques fair.

Towards the last quarter of the nineteenth century, with

Plate 3/6. English lignum vitae engine-turned 'York' tankard with original feet, handle and finial. It has an interesting early repair in silver with scalloped edges. It is useful to compare the slightly different features of the three tankards illustrated here. These three very similar tankards, as well as the three sold to Axel Vervoordt from the Hawkins collection (Plate 2/3), all have a feature that the lid opposite the handle tends to overhang the rim of the tankard significantly and sometimes has an almost pointed lip. This may, in part, be the result of repairs to the handles of some of them, but seems to be part of the design as it is evident in the silver ones from the same period. 5½in. x 5¼in.

the growth and development of the Arts and Crafts Movement in Britain, there was an increasing interest in the 'Antique' and hand-made objects, which gave birth to many copies and reproductions of early styles, which are, however, rarely confused with the originals.

Your interest may be in the changing style of goblets from 1660, it may be in the range of vessels used for drinking, it may be in the more exotic vessels such as pap boats, collapsible travelling beakers, vessels made from named and dated trees or ships being broken up or it may be trying to find examples of identical styles in multiple different materials: silver, brass, pewter or different woods. The possibilities are huge and fascinating but please, if you become an expert in a particular field, publish the information so we can all learn from your experience.

Plate 3/8. An early 17th century lignum vitae goblet with beautifully preserved elaborate and deep rose engine turning on the foot. The elegant stem has two turned discs framing the ball knopped stem supporting a plain undecorated bowl in well figured lignum selected for the grain. 6½in. x 4in.

Plate 3/7 (Opposite). Very fine and rare English rose engine turned lignum vitae goblet with a scalloped contemporary silver rim which, not unusually, is without hallmarks. When only a small amount of silver was used it was not worth sending to the Assay Office. This is a piece of remarkable quality and special elegance with its decorated knop, particularly intricate patterns of decoration and fine patination. Second quarter 17th century. 6in. x 3in.

Plate 3/9. A rare English silver mounted lobed lignum vitae standing cup with a large silver print engraved with a crown and the initials C and JS. The base of the bowl has the residual memory of engine turning and the cup is raised on a moulded foot and short stem. It is most unusual to find lobed vessels of the type and they are commonly regarded as a 'tour de force' of the turner's art. Second half 17th century. 4¼in. x 5in. across the bowl.

Plate 3/9A. Interior.

Plate 3/10A. Close–up detail.

Plate 3/10. A particularly fine English cup beautifully preserved with linear geometric scratch-carved decoration entirely characteristic of a group of cups. The base shows fine pole lathe turning and branded initials 'AR'. A few other examples are known, such as the one in the Scarborough Museum. These date from c.1600 and are normally found to be in pearwood. This example is particularly remarkable for the generosity of the central disc knop to the stem. 8¾in. x 3¾in.

Plate 3/10B. Base.

Plate 3/12. An early English pearwood goblet c.1620 with an interesting knopped baluster stem and decorated with incised roundels, in common with other pieces from this period, around the rim and foot. 8¼in. x 5¼in.

Plate 3/11. A rare English fruitwood or sycamore goblet with a flat knop and a high stepped foot, all with interesting incised decoration. Compare this foot with the one from the Fardon Collection shown in Plate 3/22. Second quarter 17th century. 6½in. x 3¼in.

Plate 3/11A. Under surface of the base of the goblet shown in Plate 3/11 to show the concave bottom with the pole lathe turning marks.

Plate 3/13. A late 17th century English cedarwood standing cup and cover with a nest of eleven graduated dipper cups and the centrepiece. The cover has an acorn finial, the stem a classic knop above a lovely domed foot. The difference in colour and patination between the cup and dippers is due to the the differences in wear and exposure to light. 10⅓in. x 5¼in.

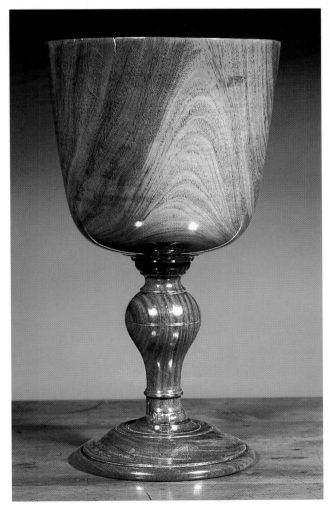

Plate 3/14. A fine and rare English lignum vitae goblet or chalice of large proportions, raised on a baluster stem with a slightly tapering bowl above. Early 17th century. 12in. x 5in.

Plate 3/15. Wonderfully shaped English fruitwood goblet from 1670-80 with a bold knopped stem typical of the Restoration period. It has excellent colour but a repaired foot. 7⅓in. x 5in.

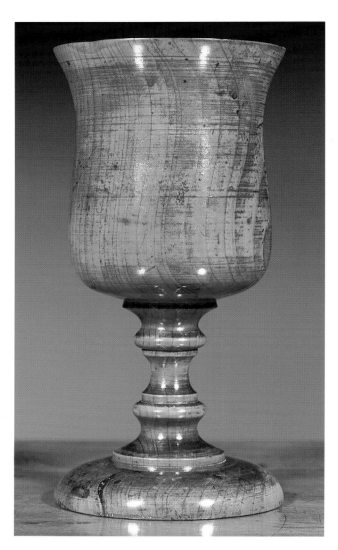

Plate 3/16. A late 18th century English yew or cedarwood goblet with a tulip shaped bowl above an interesting double knop and slightly domed foot. It has a particularly rich colour. 7in. x 3½in.

Plate 3/17A.

Plate 3/17 (Opposite). Large English pearwood goblet from the first half of the 17th century with fine colour and patination, and a wonderful domed base. This goblet is very similar to that illustrated in plate 6 of the Evan-Thomas catalogue, 1921. The semi-circular arcades and cross-hatched decoration is entirely typical of this group of cups. This also has a characteristic feature of many high quality pieces in its deep concavity under the foot. This with the meticulous turning is shown in Plate 3/17A.

Plate 3/18. Left. A superb English lignum vitae domestic goblet, turned largely from the sapwood, the generous bowl supported by an interesting decoratively turned stem and standing on a flared foot with ring-turned incised decoration to the outside edges. Second half 17th century. 5¾in. x 4in.

Right. English maple cup with a slightly tapered bowl, a rounded knop on a good stem and with a slightly small foot, all with ring-turned incised decoration. The foot has a concave base and is engraved with the initials MC twice. c.1660. 6½in. x 3¼in.

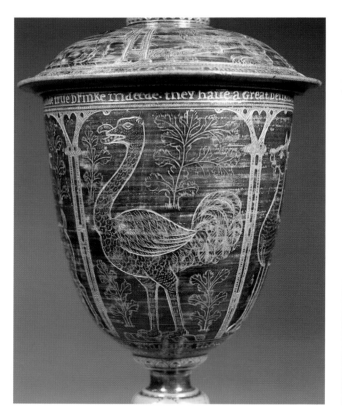

Plate 3/19. Remarkable, exceedingly rare and astonishingly well preserved armorial James I standing cup and cover in pearwood and dated 1621. The incised burned decoration and lettering has been executed with meticulous skill and artistry. The bowl is divided decoratively into four sections, each showing a mythological beast, with additional foliage in residual spaces thought to represent the arms of various families. These are an ostrich holding a horseshoe in its beak, a hart with a crown round its neck apparently attached to a long tassel, a standing unicorn on the dated panel, a phoenix rising from the flames above a coronet. Above and below are inscriptions reading as follows: (rim) 'The pure in heart do finde true drinke indeede: they have a great delight Gods word to heare: his spirit ther by their soules doth.' (bottom of the bowl) 'Doth truely feede: assuring them of endless joy most dear.' (second line) 'This good assurance in this lyfe they finde'. The pillared and knopped decorated stem rises from a domed foot with alternating flower patterns and with an additional inscription reading: 'Being sound regenerate and renewed in minde: few such ther be many in sinne are blind'. The close fitting domed lid with an overhanging rim has a further circumferential inscription, four panels with beasts and finally a damaged, decorated removable finial. The beasts are an elephant, a salamander (or is this a griffin?), a different unicorn, and possibly a dog. The inscription reads 'Accept my smalle gifte and good will: desiring God to bless you still: and send you many years of joy by walking in the living way.' The missing part of the finial was, by comparison with other known examples of these cups, an elegant pinnacle containing a spice cup in its hollow knop (see cup dated 1614 in the Burrell Collection and another in the Victoria and Albert Museum).

Plate 3/20. English armorial James I standing cup in pearwood and dated 1628. The incised burned decoration and mythological beasts seem to come from the same hand as Plates 3/19 and 3/21. This example has no cover and has a replacement stem and foot. The bowl is divided decoratively into three cartouches separated by pillars with a heart below the rim. Each section contains a different mythological beast thought to represent different families. A stag surrounded by plants (said to be the crest of Lisle) with the date 1628. A wyvern holding in its mouth a right hand or glove couped at the wrist with an arrow emerging from its mouth and inscribed 'God Save our king'. This is said to be the crest of William Herbert, third Earl of Pembroke. The last shows a phoenix rising from the flames above a coronet said to be the crest of Edward Seymour, Earl of Hertford. The delicacy and finesse of the decoration is remarkable. It is difficult to imagine that it was burnt in without previous scratch carving. Examination of two of the examples in the British Museum is particularly interesting as they clearly reveal incised decoration without any burning, proving that carving was the first step in their decoration and somehow these two were only partly treated pyrographically subsequently. The origin and purpose of these armorial cups remain mysterious.

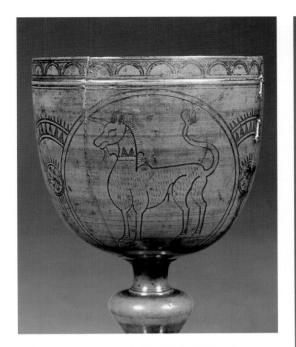

Plate 3/21. Rare early 17th century English standing cup with three heraldic animals in inscribed circles below a rim inscribed with half roundels. The animals are scratch carved within circular cartouches in charmingly primitive form. All three have simple crowns round their necks. They appear to be a unicorn and two other animals that are difficult to identify, though one might be a stag – all with well endowed genitalia. Between the inscribed cartouches are decorations which one suspects have significance though this is difficult to discern now. The piece is undated and has no armorial section. The slightly domed foot flares out from the knopped baluster stem. Neither the foot nor the stem have any decoration and there is no inscription in the base. The cup has old wire repairs. 8in. x 4in.

Plate 3/22. This goblet is an amazing survivor from the last quarter of the 16th century or the first quarter of the 17th. It was previously in the John Fardon Collection, and is illustrated incidentally in Chinnery, page 259. This again has a deeply concave bottom (see Plate 3/24). 6½in. x 3½in.

Plate 3/23. An English domestic fruitwood goblet with wonderful turning, a domed foot and concave base. The wear on the knop and the base of the cup has, over the years, gently eroded the tooling marks from the lathe. These features make it a highly collectable object. A date of 1641 has been very crudely burnt into the bowl and this looks to be a late addition. The style of the pyramidal foot and bell-shaped bowl suggests a date earlier in the 17th century, probably c.1620. 5¼in. x 3¼in.

Plate 3/24. This shows the bases of the two previous goblets, illustrating the concave turning to the underside of both and the marvellous definition of the pole lathe tooling marks.

Plate 3/25. A pair of English fruitwood goblets c.1730–40 with original period painting. It is exceedingly rare to have such high quality painting preserved on English treen. Painting was probably considerably more frequent in the past on fine pieces of treen and has been washed off in use. Minor residual traces of paint or gilding are not infrequently found on other pieces, if looked for carefully, though very rarely so complete and well preserved. See also Plate 19/17. 5¼in. x 3in.

Plate 3/26. This is a very rare and remarkable survivor, in amazing condition, of a plane posset cup from the second quarter of the 17th century. Another example was illustrated in the Evan-Thomas exhibition catalogue of 1921, plate 9, and a further more elaborate one in Pinto, plate 53F. 3½in. x 4½in.

Plate 3/27. English walnut steeple footed goblet. This currently looks unbalanced and small holes around the rim suggest there was originally a silver rim which would have restored the balance and given a more acceptable appearance to this cup. There is wonderful patination and colour on the foot. c.1650 or earlier. This piece has the wide, generous bowl commonly associated with master salts and an unusually high, bold steeple foot. It is difficult to be certain of its original purpose, but the thin lip turning and evidence of a silver mount lead me to favour the concept that it was a goblet rather than a salt. 5¼in. x 3¼in.

Plate 3/28. English goblet probably in laburnum on a generous baluster stem. The photograph shows off the grain particularly well. First half 18th century. 7½in. x 3¾in.

Plate 3/29. Large English laburnum chalice from the third quarter of the 17th century. The inverted cones above and below the round knop are a typical ecclesiastical style for most of Northern Europe. 9¼in. x 4¼in.

Plate 3/30 (Opposite). Very finely turned English walnut standing cup which might have been made as a chalice. Fine turning and other features suggest an early date of c.1700,. It has excellent colour and patination, particularly on the foot. 8½in. x 3¼in.

Plate 3/31. Although not strictly treen because it is not made from turned wood, the carving and wonderful faded colour on this mounted coconut goblet was so sensational, and of such high quality, that it was irresistible. The Fishmongers Company were unable to help clarify the significance of the fish and research with the College of Arms has failed to provide certain identification of the arms. They are not the arms of Queen Anne, which would have had the first three quarters as found here but the detail in the fourth quarter (bottom right), a repetition of those in the first (top left) – England impaling Scotland. The Arms of Hanoverian George I have a rather complex detailed pattern in the fourth quarter but are otherwise identical to Anne's and those found here in the first three quarters. The problem, therefore, is the identification of this fourth quarter. The College of Arms suggests it may have been made for a family with Jacobean sympathies who had fish in their family arms (symbolically relating them to the fisherman St. Peter) and for whom it was imprudent for the engraver to complete the specifically Hanoverian quarter. He therefore replaced it with a rather simplified version of the whole. The College suggests therefore it may have been made for an exiled Jacobite family in the early 18th century. The identity of the woman in the oval cartouche remains unknown. The style of the hair and the low neck may suggest a slightly later date. If anyone can throw further light on these speculations please write to the publisher. 6½in. x 3in.

Plate 3/32 (Left). An early 19th century English laburnum goblet of fine colour and patination and of generous proportions in common with large glass tavern rummers of the same period. 5in. x 3¾in.

Plate 3/33 (Right). An English goblet in well-figured lignum vitae of chalice shape with a flat knop and foot. There is a 17th century silver precedent for this design. This example may be 17th or 18th century. 5¾in. x 3in.

Plate 3/34. A pair of late 18th century English yew wood goblets with well defined feet and decoratively turned stems, supporting bowls with bands of ring-turned decoration taking inspiration from the Renaissance period. Last quarter 18th century. 6⅛in. x 3in. A cedar goblet with a stylised fan motif carving to the underside of the bowl, made from a specimen piece of cedar. The goblet bears a hand-written inscription on the underside of the foot without which one might have been tempted to attribute an earlier date to this piece on stylistic grounds. c.1845. The inscription reads 'The wood of which this goblet is formed was cut from one of the cedars on Mount Lib—— in 1842 by Thomas Tardrew when in his travels with Lord Castlereagh.' 6in. x 3½in.

Plate 3/35. An exquisitely turned English sycamore small drinking bowl reminiscent of a dipper cup though it has a short foot. It has an oriental feel and dates from the mid-18th century when chinoiserie was high fashion. 2¼in. x 3⅛in. at rim. Pole lathe turned rather wide sycamore goblet from the Darton Collection with burnt stylised line and berry decoration which implies a Welsh origin. c.1780. 3¾in. x 3¾in.

Plate 3/36. 1. English pearwood tulip shaped goblet on a high knopped stem. It is very similar to the oak one in Plate 3/40, 4. c.1900. Despite its youth this has a lovely feel. 7in. x 3¼in. **2.** English fruitwood goblet from the second half of the 19th century with good patination. 7¾in. x 3in. **3.** Rather heavy English rustic fruitwood goblet c.1780 showing residual influences from the designs of 17th century ecclesiastical chalices. 6¾in. x 3¼in. **4.** Early 19th century English walnut goblet made from a well selected piece of wood with good grain. 6½in. x 3¼in.

Plate 3/37. A simply turned 18th century English fruit-wood (possibly plum) goblet of classic shape with stunning colour and patination. 5in. x 3in.

Plate 3/38 (Opposite, above). 1. English silver rimmed lignum vitae goblet (c.1700) from Sir Ambrose Heal's Collection sold at Christie's 5.7.95, lot 779. The concave recess under the foot (not shown) is one of the hallmarks of good quality. 3¾in. x 3¼in. **2.** Pair of pearwood goblets (c.1790), probably English. No patination as they had to be stripped of their old hopelessly congealed varnish which hid their merit. This is not an uncommon shape in various woods. 4½in. x 2½in. **3.** English early 18th century laburnum goblet with a great foot. 3¼in. x 2¾in. **4.** English early 18th century applewood goblet with good colour and similar turning to **1.** 4¼in. x 3¼in. **5.** English fruitwood goblet (c.1760) with a wide bowl and knopped stem balanced by a wide flared foot. 5in. x 4⅜in. **6.** Late 18th century yew goblet with a particularly comfortable feel, fine colour and patination. Very tactile piece. This is quite a modest goblet but looks special because of its shape and feel. 4in. x 3in.

Plate 3/39 (Opposite). 1. A pair of late 18th century French boxwood goblets, each with a generous domed foot and plain cylindrical stem. 5¼in. x 2½in. **2.** Pair of English walnut goblets (c.1800) with fine pole lathe turning and interesting individual differences typical of hand-turned objects. The patination has been spoiled by over cleaning. 5¾in. x 2½in. **3.** English laburnum goblet of the last quarter of the 19th century with a good base, colour and patination. 4½in. x 3in. **4.** Small English fruitwood goblet (c.1800) with good colour and patination. 4½in. x 2¼in. **5.** English goblet, possibly apple. This is of indeterminate date as it has no distinguishing features. 5in. x 2½in. **6.** English rich fruity coloured ash goblet with wild grain and old varnish. The marvellous bun foot has the perfect profile of a bun foot from a piece of William and Mary furniture. c.1700. 5¼in. x 2¾in.

Plate 3/40 (Above). 1. Oak goblet from the last quarter of the 19th century that could well be Scottish. Warm colour. The deep line decoration on the foot is a good guide to a 19th century origin, particularly if it is deep as here. 5¾in. x 4¼in. **2.** Rather crude English birch goblet, c.1840. This has a rather bad colour and shows evidence of having been cleaned off except for the underside of the base (not shown) which has considerably more richness. 5½in. x 3¾in. **3.** English crudely turned 19th century chestnut goblet that lacks finesse and has the sharp incised line decoration on the body and a fat stem that are markers to the 19th century. 6in. x 3½in. **4.** English oak tulip shaped goblet on a high knopped stem. The style is rather mixed, with possible Art Nouveau influence suggesting a date in the last quarter of the 19th century. The base carries a piece of paper inscribed as follows: 'This vase is made out of the main beam over the captains cabin of H.M.S. "Caladonia" which was afterwards called the "Dreadnought" which was broken up in Chatham Dockyard in June 1875'. Compare this with the one of very similar style, Plate 3/36, 1. 7½in. x 3½in. **5.** A well-figured English elm goblet. A robust generous vessel. 19th century. **6.** A good piece of oak was selected to make this honey coloured English oak goblet of about 1870 which is very characteristic of its time. 5¼in. x 3in. **7.** This is a good working provincial English goblet in fruitwood, c.1820, with good proportions to its base and of quite good colour. 5⅓in. x 4⅔in. **8.** English early 19th century respectable but unexciting walnut goblet. 4½in. x 3in

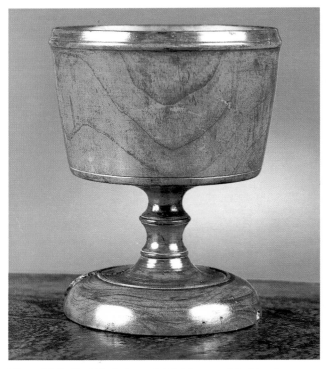

Plate 3/41. English fruitwood drinking vessel lacking its cover. Its surface and patination are undistinguished. Probably dates from the second half of the 18th century.

Plate 3/42. An 18th century staved and willow bound 'snake tankard' with the handle in the shape of a serpent made from a single piece of root. Possibly Irish. With handle 7in. x 4½in.

Plate 3/43. An 18th century stained oak coopered tankard with ash bindings. The shape is similar to those found in Scandinavian countries but this may have originated in Scotland or the north of England because neither ash nor oak are regularly used in Scandinavia. 9½in. (with handle) x 6in.

Plate 3/44. An English staved and coopered porter or ale jug in walnut fitted with original rising hinged lid and bamboo banding. The elegant line follows the style of its precedents in silver and pewter. Last quarter 18th century. 6½in. x 4¾in.

Plate 3/45. An 18th century brass-bound ale coaster of 'hour-glass' shape raised above four original brass castors. The top is carved with deep draining channels leading to a circular well. 2¾in. x 9¾in. (maximum) and 21in. long. **1.** Late 19th century oak tankard following the earlier 19th century silver and pewter shapes with an unusual mask of a man on the crest of the handle. **2.** A lignum vitae tankard c.1860 with finely turned handle and supports. **3.** Snake tankard shown in Plate 3/42.

Plate 3/46. An English early 18th century laburnum travelling cup with a silver lining and incised decoration. See Pinto plate 39 and two in the V. & A. for similar cups. 3¼in. x 1¾in.

Plate 3/47. English walnut stirrup cup with animal heads as feet – a sheep, hound and a third animal of unidentifiable origin. Probably from the last quarter of the 18th century. 4¾in. x 3½in.

Plate 3/48. Two beakers. Left. 18th century English fruitwood beaker. 3¾in. x 2½in. Right. Early 19th century English beaker in elm which was probably cleaved. 5½in. x 2in.

Plate 3/49. A rare 19th century beechwood toddy or tumbler holder with multiple perforations of the body and carved decoration to the rim and foot. 3in. x 2in.

Plate 3/50. Interesting early 19th century goblet taking its influence directly from glass shapes of the period, particularly in the faceting outside the base of the conical bowl. 5½in. x 2¼in.

Plate 3/51. An uncommon but not rare Scandinavian quatrefoil burr birch drinking bowl originating from the East coast of Norway. It retains substantial traces of its original paint. The form is medieval in origin, but the tight chip carving and the delicacy of its bowl date it to the mid–18th century. Initialled AI on base. 2in. x 3½in. (maximum diameter of bowl.)

Plate 3/52. The previous bowl shown with two other Scandinavian drinking vessels. The second is a Norwegian figured birch drinking bowl of a type traditionally passed down through families from generation to generation, with initials ending in 'D' for daughter and 'S' for son. On this bowl the inscriptions read 'M? EPD 1728. MMD 1751 and AMDF?OD 1761'. The bowl has been cherished and repaired with iron wire. 2in. x 4¾in. (maximum diameter of bowl). A Baltic sycamore handled cup that has been carved and not turned is included here for comparison. The handle is hooked, for hanging on to the side of a large beer bowl. First quarter 19th century.

Plate 3/53. A remarkable whistling cup in walnut dated 1704 and initialled CWR. This is clearly very closely related to the one illustrated in Pinto (plate 38) from the Somerset County Museum at Taunton Castle. That one is inscribed with a short poem with the name Iohn Watson 1695. The example illustrated has both date and initials as well as the additional feature of the caged ball. The whistle in the end is said to have been used to order a refill and may be the origin of the phrase 'wet your whistle'.

Plate 3/54. English red walnut beaker with simple bands developed from wassail bowls but now without a foot. c.1740. 3½in. x 3¼in.

Plate 3/55 (Below). 1. English pole lathe turned beaker, probably in laburnum, with single incised line decoration to rim and base. Mid-19th century. 3¾in. x 2¼in. **2.** Another English pole lathe turned beaker in fruitwood that has become pleasingly oval in shape. First half 19th century. 3½in. x 1¾in. **3.** English early 19th century travelling glass case in fruitwood with its original hand-blown beaker. The variation in its surface coloration, produced by handling and use, considerably adds to its attraction. 3¾in. x 2½in.

Plate 3/56 (Bottom). A pair of English laburnum collapsible travelling cups with their case. They are meticulously turned to ensure they don't leak. One is shown erect and the other collapsed. 19th century,

Plate 3/57. English sycamore cup and cover with fantastic colour and well defined turning to base. Probably c.1680. Though it has been suggested this may have been related to drinking its use is uncertain. The lid now doesn't fit tightly, otherwise one would think it was a spice pot. 5in. x 3¾in.

CHAPTER 4

Irish Drinking Vessels

Plate 4/1. My wife with the methers unearthed in a reserve collection of treen.

The acknowledged and sought after specifically Irish wooden drinking vessels are the lámhóg and the mether. They were thought to be in common use throughout the country so it is surprising that so few have been preserved, the mether being even less common than the lámhóg. Historically, commonplace drinking vessels were both cut from the solid and coopered. While some still exist they tend to be crude and simple and none has been encountered.

The largest study on methers, which includes some information on lámhógs, is the thesis by Bernard Estridge 'A Catalogue of Irish Methers' (1983) from the Department of Archaeology, The Queen's University of Belfast. The Irish National Museum in Dublin has about sixty-five methers while the Ulster Museum has twelve

and other Irish museums even fewer. It is interesting that he found no previous study of methers. In Great Britain examples can be seen in the Burrell Collection in Glasgow and the reserve collections in the British Museum in London and the York Museums.

A mether, in Irish 'meader', is a handled wooden quadrangular drinking cup or vessel which has been carved from a single solid piece of wood, except for the bottom which is a separate and independent entity inserted into the base of the vessel. The handles form an integral part of the vessel, that is, they have been carved from the solid, and are not separate additions. Drinking was done from the corners. There are two known types, the two- and four-handled. The four-handled ones sometimes have handles that extend down to become legs,

Plate 4/2. Irish mether of characteristic shape with four handles, a square rim and round base with incised pokerwork decoration, almost certainly made from willow in spite of the label which states 'Ancient Irish Mether of maple. Crockers Sale. Bateman Col.[ection]'. Date unknown. These form a fascinating part of Irish folklore and are known to date from the Middle Ages although it is now impossible to date individual items accurately. They are all largely considered to pre-date 1600. 6¾in. x 3⅛in.

Plate 4/3. 17th or 18th century Irish lámhóg in willow of typical form with the colour of a light suntan. Its interesting old repair is shown in detail in Plate 17/3. 7¾in. x 5in.

Plate 4/4. 1. A small Irish lámhóg, unusually with five turned bands of decoration with a further three just at the foot. 19th century? This comes from the Sir Ambrose Heal Collection, lot 770, sold at Christie's on 5.7.95. **2.** A larger Irish lámhóg, probably from the 18th century, in willow with a particularly pale glistening almost ivory colour. It has a single subtle turned band of decoration above the handle. Its long split has been repaired with spliced willow and is shown in detail in Plate 17/2.

raising the vessel off the table. The top of a mether is always rectangular and larger than the rest of the body or base which may become circular. Half of the methers examined in his thesis had some decoration to the body, usually broad and scorched.

To indicate the lack of knowledge and awareness that exists about methers is an interesting experience my wife and I had at a renowned and excellent museum. They kindly allowed us to view their reserve collection of treen. Having searched through numerous well labelled and packed boxes of treasures we came across a rather 'end of bin' box with a number of unlabelled objects. Can you imagine our amazement when we found a galaxy of methers, the current staff being unaware of their existence or significance (Plate 4/1)?

The lámhóg, a turned vessel which could only be made on a pole lathe, is entirely different from the mether. It is a circular downward tapering vessel which flares out at the base with an integral handle that it was possible to turn because of the reciprocating movement of this type of lathe. They vary in height from 5½in. to 8½in. While some are plain most have two incised lines as decoration and most were made from willow. They were used as common drinking vessels in Irish taverns well into the middle of this century and some were exported to inns in the West of England and Wales.

Estridge in his thesis gives no information about dating either type of vessel but does warn that in the past there has been a some faking of Irish antiquities.

CHAPTER 5

Scottish Drinking Vessels

Plate 5/1. A large Scottish quaich with coopered cedar staves, silver rim, a silver ring round the base as well as silver mounted handles. The central silver boss is very finely engraved with a crown and thistle as well as the date 1707 – the year of the Treaty of Union between Scotland and England. The motto reads: 'Nemo me Impune Lacesset' which was the motto of the Kings of Scotland and translates as 'No one provokes me with impunity'. This is very similar to one shown in plate 3 in Evan-Thomas and another in the Burrell Collection, though this has three handles. The date is probably contemporary. The simulated binding is from a solid piece of wood turned as a ring and then attached to the staves, remarkably with wooden pins which are clearly visible in the third picture. 2½in. x 6½in. or 9¾in. across the handles.

I n earlier times Scottish society was very orientated round drinking. In this it was similar to Scandinavia and the study of their social history reveals the importance of drink in their ceremonial lives in particular.

Before discussing particular Scottish drinking vessels their definition needs to be stated. There are two groups of vessels, the bicker family and the quaiches. Bickers are specifically Scottish and may be defined as straight-sided vessels of bucket form. They were usually built with alternating staves of sycamore and alder that had been steeped in peat bogs to stain them dark brown. Two staves, usually light sycamore ones, were extended horizontally to form concave handles. The staves were feathered together miraculously accurately, being made, it

is believed, only with simple tools. They were then bound with willow. Really large bickers were called cogs or coggies, the difference being only one of size.

A piggin is a straight-sided circular vessel usually but not always coopered with an upstanding short lug to act as a handle for use both for drinking and as a ladle.

A luggie is a vessel identical to a piggin except that one stave is longer, extending upwards to form a bigger lug or handle presumably to enable it to be used as a ladle more effectively.

A quaich may be defined as a shallow curved bowl for drinking spirits, usually with two handles. The small ones were for individual use while the larger ones were for ceremonial use or passing round the table as with loving cups. A silver engraved boss is common in quaiches, their complexity being related to their ceremonial importance. The four-handled or lugged ones were largely made after 1800 and for domestic and not ceremonial use.

Plate 5/2. Six Scottish quaiches and a bicker of various sizes and types. Quaiches are usually rather shallow curved bowls while bickers are deeper and straight sided. Three quaiches **(2, 4 and 6)** have no handles as such but vestigial lugs that are too small to be functional handles. **6** in sycamore is inscribed 'Foster Forbes' and has remarkable patination and colour. **7** has a silver base plate inscribed 'The Duchess of Athole to her nephew Baron Poellnitz Dunkeld 1840'. **5** is particularly finely pole lathe turned and appears to be of an earlier date. **3** is a typical bicker with alternating staves of sycamore and alder which has been stained dark brown by steeping the wood in a peat bog. The technical skill of the maker in producing such a perfect and water-tight fit with the 'feathering' is quite remarkable, and shown in detail in the close-up. The staves are held together by tightly woven bands of willow. These remarkable examples of craftsman's art are usually dated to the 18th and 19th centuries.

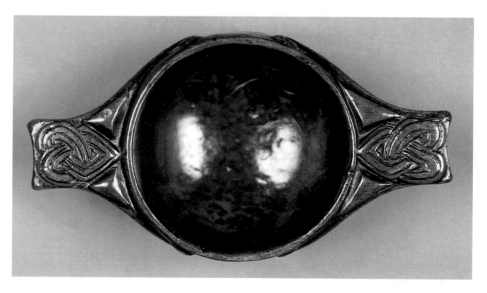

Plate 5/3. Quaich to show fine carving of intertwined hearts on the handles and seen better in the next plate, with elegant scrolling on to the body. Possibly early 18th century. 1¼in. x 4½in.

Plate 5/4. Three quaiches, the third being the one from the previous plate. The first is of rosewood and 19th century. The second is of yew with thistles on the curved handles and inscribed 'Squat. as. c.' The extra work that has gone into the handles as well as their generosity indicates this had a more important ceremonial function. The other two were probably personal.

Plate 5/5. A selection of three Scottish quaiches, all from the first half of the 19th century and carved with a basket weave pattern. The first has a quatrefoil form, the largest is of oak and the one on the right is laburnum. 2in. x 1⅜in. 2⅜in. x 3in. 1¼in. x 1¼in.

Plate 5/6. 1. An 18th century Scottish walnut quaich turned and carved from solid walnut with four rather than the more usual two lugs. 1½in. x 4½in. at the rim with handles. **2.** An 18th century laburnum Scottish coopered quaich with willow banding and a copper band to the foot. 1½in. x 6in. with handles. **3.** A small personal quaich with silver bands to the rim and foot. 19th century.

Plate 5/7. A selection of four Scottish bickers and one piggin (unusually with two lugs rather than one), all with alternately coloured staves and bound with willow. One is unusual being bound with a silver rim and another is unusually small.

Plate 5/8. A selection of three Scottish luggies, the centre one bound with tinplate as well as willow. The left-hand one bound in ash may be referred to as a piggin as its handle is shorter. Sizes with handles 6in. x 4in., 6½in. x 4in., 6½in. x 4¼in.

Plate 5/9 (Top). A selection of three 19th century small drinking vessels very reminiscent of Scottish bickers, all with turned decoration to simulate willow binding. **1.** Beech. 3in. x 3¾in. **2.** Oak with a small handle like a piggin. 3¾in. x 3¾in. **3.** Pollard oak. 3½in. x 3in.

Plate 5/10 (Above). 1. A small Scottish tankard bound with willow with alternating staves of light and dark wood (alder and sycamore). There is some chip carved decoration to the lid. c.1800. **2.** A particularly rich nutty brown coloured Scottish sycamore quaich initialled ID on the base. A good working everyday drinking vessel with a hole to hang it on a hook. Reputedly also some drinking bowls were carried by their owners by being attached to the belt. c.1800. 2in. x 3¾in. across the bowl.

Plate 5/11 (Right). Unusual Scottish beaker made in the same manner as a bicker with alternating coloured staves, feathered together and bound in willow. 19th century. 3¾in. x 2½in.

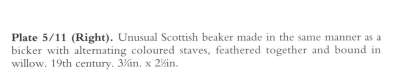

CHAPTER 6

Casters, Muffineers and Dredgers

There does not seem to be a clear distinction between the supposed function of containers with pierced lids – casters, muffineers and dredgers – nor whether a particular shape or size should give that piece one specific name rather than one of the others. It may be that the name dredger should be confined to 'casters' with handles. What is clear is that this type of container was devised for sprinkling sugar, various peppers and spices – particularly cinnamon over food generally and muffins or hot buttered toast in particular. The best cinnamon came from Ceylon but commercial production didn't develop until the mid-eighteenth century. Towards the end of the eighteenth century casters for sugar became less fashionable, being replaced by sugar bowls and baskets, but continued to be made for peppers and spices.

The tradition that the shapes of treen objects followed the changing styles in silver is particularly strong with muffineers and casters. Though casters for sugar have continued to be made in silver till the present time, the fashion of eating muffins with cinnamon or pepper was relatively short lived in the latter half of the eighteenth century. It seems that many of the small wooden muffineers could have been made from about the end of the first quarter of the eighteenth century into the beginning of the nineteenth century. These, which are becoming more difficult to find, are usually 5in to 5½in. high and made from sycamore, boxwood or fruitwood. Two defects are unfortunately rather common. The first is splitting of the foot and the second splitting of the pierced top, possibly due to excessive attempts to tighten the screw.

Earlier examples, often made from lignum vitae with walrus tusk or other bone encircling rings and occasionally, in the earliest, ivory, are rather larger, being 5in to 8in. high. These are very difficult to find.

The specific function, whether for sugar, spice or pepper, must have been clear at the time, as one rule we can latch on to is that objects were made for specific purposes, even if that is obscure or debatable to us now. The problem, therefore, is whether there are clues in the design or known habits of the time. The plethora of muffineers of, very generally, similar design and shape (and over fifty are illustrated here) implies a common function which does temporarily seem to be related to the availability of cinnamon in particular, as well as the fashion of the times. Food was heavily spiced and peppered so containers for these may have survived with some relationship to the frequency they were made and used for their specific purpose.

In the seventeenth century sugar came in loaves and had to be cut up, using special cutters which have survived in profusion, and then ground to a powder, presumably in a mortar or mortar grinder. The size of the holes in muffineers tends to be large in the early lignum specimens which were presumably designed for sugar. Silver casters often came in sets of three, clearly designed for sugar, peppers (several varieties were available) and spices, yet the size of the holes is not different and tends towards the generous size. Occasionally a 'blind' caster is found in these sets for mustard. Peppers and spices were expensive and would run freely through small holes such as found in the large number of small muffineers shown here. The evidence therefore is somewhat conflicting and the reader is left to draw his own conclusions as to their exact usage.

In silver, lighthouse casters were the earliest shape, being made from about 1660 up to about 1705. Cylindrical with vertical sides, the body encircled with a narrow band of moulding, these had a spreading moulded foot and a pierced, often domed top, with a knop finial. One in lignum vitae in this style was sold in the W.J. Shepherd Collection at Sotheby's (30.11.83, lot 748). Plate 6/1 shows a silver and treen example together.

At the end of the seventeenth century a pear (also called vase) shape became fashionable, often with a rib round the widest part, a moulded or collared foot and essentially no stem. These date particularly from approximately 1700–1725/30. Plates 6/2 and 6/3 show examples in lignum vitae.

From about the start of the second quarter of the seventeenth century in silver, the upper part of the body became concave, a feature which was popular for the next thirty years, and is often also referred to as vase shaped (just to make life confusing) and developed a stem in the middle of the century. This concavity could be so pronounced that the upper part of the bowl was almost horizontal. From about 1750 the lower part of the body merging into the stem often had a double curve, referred to as ogee shaped, gradually becoming more elongated. This coincides with the development, in the Industrial Revolution, of cheap spinning techniques for silver rather

Plate 6/1. A contemporary silver lighthouse caster of classic traditional form, shown alongside a period c.1690 English lignum example. Whilst the silver one is a copy it retains the cylindrical body with bands of ribbed decoration and slightly flared foot, raised turned finial and decorative piercing in common with its ancestors.

Plate 6/2. 1. A modern silver caster derivative of 1690-1710 design to show the development of shape and style. **2.** English lignum vitae early 18th century muffineer with stepped domed foot, straight sided 'lighthouse' top but with replaced finial. The form is transitional between the silver one on its left and that on its right hallmarked for London 1708. 7¼in. x 2¼in. **3.** Silver caster hallmarked 1708. **4.** See Plate 6/3 (4). **5.** A modern silver caster derivative of c.1710-20 shape to compare with the lignum examples.

Plate 6/3. 1. An English lignum vitae muffineer with marine ivory finial and band. The foot is small and closely stepped. The pierced holes are unexpectedly large. The reason is not apparent but it is likely this was designed for sugar and not spices. c.1700-20. 7in. x 2in. **2.** English fruitwood and sycamore muffineer with a horn finial of a particularly slim and elegant shape. Last quarter 18th century. 6¼in. x 2¼in. **3.** English lignum vitae muffineer of substantially similar style and date but without any holes on the actual dome. This has a similarly stepped foot to 1. 1700-10. 5in. x 2in. **4.** English lignum vitae muffineer with marine ivory band and finial (partly missing). The overall shape is more generous and the domed wider foot is more substantial than in the other lignum examples shown which makes the whole object more elegant. c.1700-20 6. 6½in. x 2½in.

A group of three muffineers of traditional pear-shaped form sadly now lacking finials. Whether designed as toys, tradesman's samples or details from a dolls' house remains speculative but they show genuine evidence of age and have very fine turning. c.1700-20. Approx. 1⅝in.

Plate 6/4. Unusual English straight-sided muffineer with old varnish giving a variegated slightly crinkled appearance. Probably early 19th century. 6¼in. x 1¾in.

Plate 6/5. Two muffineers described elsewhere to compare with the third on the right, an English fruitwood muffineer of generous low bellied pear shape with a simple ball finial. c.1780. 5½in. x 2in. The middle one has a particularly variegated surface patination.

than hammering. This shape, referred to as an inverted pear, was common into the next century but has not been seen in any of the wooden examples shown here, though some may have shown lengthening of the stem. This contrasts with other metals and an example of the inverted pear muffineers in silver (dated 1767), brass and pewter are shown in Plate 6/7. There is no obvious explanation for the failure to develop the ogee shape in wood which would not have presented any technical problems. The treen equivalent may have been a gradual change in the shape of the bowl which became more conical, as shown in Plate 6/7. The neo-classical urn shape developed from 1780 onwards.

In silver, smaller casters about 5in. high were often called (spice) muffineers while the larger sugar casters were superseded in the last quarter of the century by sugar bowls and baskets with sifter spoons.

Another style in silver, particularly for spice, was 4in. to 5in. high and had a bun pierced top. This does not seem

Plate 6/6. English sycamore sifter probably designed for sugar but also used with many other powders including flour. These were made extensively from the 17th to 20th centuries, both with and without handles. This example is late but is pole lathe turned and can reasonably be dated to the mid-19th century. It is shown with a muffineer to give an impression of its size. 4½in. x 2¾in.

Plate 6/7. Two rows of muffineers. The top row shows an example in silver (5¼in. high and dated 1767) which provides the model for the pewter and brass. In spite of reviewing a very large number of muffineers for this book, no treen examples were found with this particular ogee form. This is puzzling as the shape is not difficult to turn in wood and muffineers were being made throughout this period in the four different materials.

Clearly the ogee shape in treen never caught on. The reason for this is a complete mystery that warrants further study. A treen example from a similar period is included for comparison. The bottom row is an attempt to show the development and degree of variation within a group of urn-shaped muffineers which span about sixty years from 1760 to 1820.

Plate 6/8 (Opposite). Top row. 1. Unusual beech wood muffineer with a smoothly stepped high foot and onion finial not obviously derived from any well-known silver examples. 19th century. 6in. x 2¼in. **2.** A boxwood, possibly French, muffineer of unusually large size and generous proportions. Mid-18th century. 6in. x 3½in. **3.** English burr box muffineer. It has an interesting old repair to its top but unfortunately some vandal has cut off the flange from the foot. Even if it had been damaged at some stage in its turbulent life, honourable scars would be much preferred to the vandal's knife. c.1725 4¾in. x 2in.
Second row. 1 and 7. Two English sycamore muffineers, both with rare poker work decoration. Late 18th century. 5in. x 2¼in. and 6in. x 2½in. **2 and 6.** A pair of unusual oak muffineers with silver tops hallmarked 1800 previously in the Shepherd Collection (label numbered DIR 1637) sold at the 1983 Sotheby's sale, lot 741. 4¾in. x 2½in. **3 and 5.** Two fruitwood muffineers, both with a deep rich colour and virtually identical. Other than the pair from the Shepherd Collection, this is the

only set of twins that have appeared amongst the very large number of muffineers examined in the preparation of this book. They were bought from two entirely different sources at different times. This underlines the fact that there must have been very large numbers of turners producing muffineers as it is so rare to find twins, which is unlike our experience with some other objects. 18th century. 5¾in. x 2½in. **4.** English lighthouse muffineer with original brown paint on the body and tower but with dark blue/green round the windows which are made from glass. The foot has been replaced. This is the only example seen without the usual screw top, this one being just pushed on. We can find no precedent for this piece so it is difficult to date but may be early 18th century. 6½in. x 2in.
Bottom row. 1. Pole lathe turned 'pourer'. This is likely to be French. The uncertainty about its origins is made up for by the fact it has a satisfying deep nutty colour and is a 'feely'. c.1800. 5½in. x 2¼in. **2 to 6.** A collection of French pourers for pepper or spice. Probably all 19th century though some could be even later.

to have been a style frequently copied in wood.

Examples of the many minor variations in shape of wooden muffineers are shown in Plates 6/7 to 6/9.

Occasional muffineers, often more crudely turned, have a painted rim reminiscent of that found in some souvenir woodware so popular as Tunbridge ware. However, no examples are mentioned in either of the two main books on the subject (Brian Austen 1989, H. & E. Pinto 1970).

Virtually all the muffineers illustrated here have been pole lathe and not machine turned.

Plate 6/9. The top two rows show a group of thirteen muffineers, all different with a rather rounded body surmounted by an incised rim of varying depths which forms a collar from which the neck flares up into the unadorned lids. The body tapers rather generously into a short stem and rather domed foot. The finials tend to be similar and they are all 5in. to 5½in. high. They are made from fruitwood, box or sycamore. An occasional one has a painted band, usually in red. Their colour and patination obviously vary but can be rich and succulent.

Third row. This row of seven illustrates two tendencies. The concavity at the shoulder becomes more pronounced and sharper and secondly the body becomes more sharply tapering into the stem, particularly in the last muffineer in the row.

Bottom row. Those have an almost round body. The first is obviously the finest, with a lovely mottled surface and patination, elegant proportions and a small rounded dome above the straight sided top. The last three show a development of an increasing concavity to the shoulders.

I have not been able to draw any conclusions from these various observations but feel there is need for scholarly research on the subject. The relationship of the changing silver styles is difficult to relate directly to the treen examples except at the start of this period.

CHAPTER 7

Salt and Spice Containers

Plate 7/1. 1. Remarkable English sycamore pole lathe turned master salt of about 1600 with a wide disc shaped knop, an interesting early foot and with ancient encrustation in the bowl. All these features make this a pleasing and rare object. 5½in. x 4in. **2.** Irish yew master salt with a wonderful deep rich colour and surface probably dating from 1720 though its feel is somehow rather earlier. 5¾in. x 3¼in.

Salts

The earliest and most magnificent silver or silver gilt standing salts once adorned the tables of medieval nobles. They are symbols of a long vanished social system in which ceremony and colour reigned supreme. Rigid rules governed behaviour at dining tables and the ceremonials around and the significance of the master salt is outlined in *Three Centuries of English Domestic Silver* by B. and T. Hughes. These large master salts were often very elaborate and decorative, though the actual receptacle for the salt was small and almost insignificant. This is rather difficult to understand. Though salt was expensive it is not likely to have stretched the house-keeping money for individuals wealthy enough to own an elaborate silver master salt. Individuals may have taken a 'pinch of salt'

with wet fingers and salt anyway attracts moisture, so it is sensible to provide it in small containers to reduce waste. However, this doesn't really provide a satisfactory explanation for why the actual amount dispensed in such an expensive and magnificent receptacle was so small. The most important salt was placed in front of the Lord of the house. Other large master salts were placed at the end of the table and multiple small trencher salts put out for the use of lower ranking guests. Thus arose the common term above and below the salt, referring to an individual's social position.

The silver salt cellar was not merely a container for an essential additive to food but held this huge symbolic and ritual significance. The inventory of the plate of Edward

Plate 7/2. 1. A large rare English master salt in faded but well marked lignum vitae with a wide disc knop on a generous stem and a well balanced foot. Late 17th century. 5½in. x 5½in.

2. Elegant and finely turned salt in walnut with a shallow bowl on a good knopped stem. Very early 18th century. 5in. x 3½in.

Plate 7/3. 1. English burr oak master salt that lacks the elegance of the next example. 2¼in. deep. The turning on the bottom is not attractive but it is made from a good piece of timber and probably dates from the late 18th to the early 19th century. 5¼in. x 5½in.
2. English burr oak master salt of the mid-18th century that has rich deep glowing colour and all the elegance missing from the previous example. 2⅜in. deep. This was previously in the Darton Collection. They had bought it from a dealer in Stoke Prior,

Herefordshire after a local auction where it had attracted the attention of Barbara Pearce who at that time was writing a weekly article on antiques for the *Berrow's Worcester Journal*. She recounted, in her article of 26 September 1974 how this piece had remained for many years before the auction in the Shropshire garden of the elderly owner and that the sparrows drank from it after the rain – a remarkable example of the survival potential of burr oak even in the English climate. 4¼in. x 4¼in.

Plate 7/4. A handsome English cedar master salt from the last quarter of the 17th century with solid straight sided foot with moulded decoration to its upper side. 4½in. x 4¼in.

III taken in 1329 listed 539 salts of various types. Trencher salts were for lesser mortals but with the passage of time became standard throughout society. In silver, all salts were of the trencher type from about 1700. There are records of trencher salts being made by potters in the late seventeenth century. This historical background is given to consider the dating in a social context. By the second half of the seventeenth century the customs had completely changed. Senior members of the household dined privately and the elaborate ceremony of earlier periods was superseded. Early seventeenth century trencher salts in silver were commonly low and squat in

Plate 7/5. 1. English yew wood salt, with a shallow cup, rich nutty colour and patination. 4¼in. x 3in. **2.** Very special English yew wood salt with a wide disc shaped moulded knopped stem and an elegant bowl with a simple ring turned collar and outstanding colour and patination. c.1660. 4½in. x 2½in.

Plate 7/6 (Above). These three salts are comparable to known examples in pewter, and probably date to the first quarter of the 18th century. They are intermediate in size, between the older master salts and the later trencher salts. All have a widely flaring circular foot with an ogee profile terminating in a stepped rim which in turn rises into a flared stem with a disc turned collar.
1. English pear wood salt. Because of its magic colour this example is more pleasing than the others though otherwise similar. 4in. x 3¾in. **2.** English sycamore salt. 3¾in. 3⅞in. **3.** English sycamore salt. 3½in. x 4in.

Plate 7/7 (Left). This is a remarkable survivor from the early 17th century of a battered and well used oak salt, crawling with character and with amazing encrustations of 'gunk' in the bowl. 2½in. x 3½in.

Plate 7/8 (Below). A particularly interesting pair of English burr wood salts, possibly juniper. These have acquired marvellous movement, shrinkage and colour through careful handling and polishing over many years. These features make them highly exciting to a collector. Mid-18th century. 2⅜in. x 3in.

Plate 7/9. 1. English cedar wood salt with good turning marks on the base from the Tim Tyrer Collection. This is probably a salt but it has a rather deep bowl (almost 2in.) for one of this date. c.1800. 3½in. x 2½in. **2.** A more impressive English yew wood master salt probably from the late 18th century with a sharply cut square foot. 4½in. x 4¼in. **3.** A very good English rather dark and heavy laburnum salt. It could be dated to about 1680 but the incised decoration round the bowl is more characteristic of 1760. Whilst the overall shape owes a strong debt to 17th century forms, the incised ring decoration to the outside of the bowl suggests an 18th century origin. 3½in. x 3½in. **4.** English fruitwood bowl, possibly cherry, which seems likely to have been for salt or other condiments. It has a particularly rich colour, good turning and shrinkage. Dating is difficult with this simple form. Late 18th or early 19th century. 3½in. x 2½in. **5.** English laburnum salt with moulded foot of around 1800 with interesting and rather pleasing variation in its colour. 4in. x 3¼in. **6.** English lignum vitae master salt of the late 18th century. This is a good example of the definition of the sapwood. The stem has remnants of a disc knop now rather shrunken. Note again the square cut and then stepped foot. 4¼in. x 3¼in. **7.** Small English sycamore salt, 2¾in. in height, shown in several groups of salts to give an impression of their variation in size.

form, circular, rectangular and octagonal in shape with a multitude of moulded and faceted sides. After about 1730 the silversmiths used the newly available rolled silver to make small hemispherical bowls raised on scrolled feet — clearly a style not reproducible in wood.

Treen salts must have been used by individuals considerably lower down the social scale in general. There are however a number of salts, apparently dating from at least the 17th century, of sufficient size to be called master salts and sufficient elegance to have been more than just convenient simple containers. This spectrum is illustrated. The vast majority of the goodly collection shown here date from the mid-eighteenth century into the nineteenth century. They are of considerable interest in that there are so many different styles and forms as well as such a wide variety of woods. They are also available in sufficient numbers for an individual to make a fascinating collection without undue expense.

Plate 7/12. English sycamore pole lathe turned salt of wonderful shape with a small knop datable to 1700 on the basis of precedent in pewter. The base is also shown (above). Some wretched previous owner or dealer has ruined its colour by over cleaning and removed any vestige of patination. Very sad – a good example of what not to do with your treen.

Plate 7/10. 1. French boxwood salt with excellent colour, c.1820. 3½ x 3in. **2.** French boxwood salt with applied shellac finish to enhance and accentuate the grain. c.1880. 3¼in. x 2in. **3.** Mid–19th century cedar trencher salt. 1½in. x 2⅜in. **4.** Handsome English boxwood salt, c.1720. This follows the classic silver shape. The dark translucent honey colour and wonderful turning make this piece into one of the highest quality. 2in. x 2¼in. **5.** Small English sycamore salt 2⅜in. high shown in several groups to give an impression of the variations in size.

Plate 7/11. A good example of a 'working' Welsh salt typical of what might be found in a farmhouse or tavern. Sycamore, c.1800. 1½in. x 2¼in.

Plate 7/13.
Row 1. 1. Richly coloured and well-proportioned English yew wood salt of c.1840 with pleasing marks of pole lathe turning. 2¼in. x 2¼in. **2.** Ebony English salt with an ivory rim from the late 19th century. This is the only example shown of a whole school of objects made from these imported materials. Vanitory sets are common. Though a satisfactory design this piece is of little interest to the treen collector as ebony has a uniform flat appearance without subtlety or variation in colour. 2¼in. x 1½in. **3 and 5.** A pair of English laburnum salts, probably c.1880 though this design was made in silver between 1700-25. They are machine turned and the raised ring decoration is rather sharp. 1in. x 2¼in. **4.** English lignum vitae turner's 'tour de force' with two freely mobile rings round the stem. This is probably a salt but the bowl is rather shallow. It must be an extremely rare if not unique piece. Surface shows the 'craquelure appearance' often found on early lignum pieces. The date is uncertain but it probably dates from the 17th century. 2in. x 2½in. **6.** Lignum vitae salt made largely from the sapwood which accounts for the light colour. It is rare to find a piece turned mainly from the sapwood. The clue it is lignum is the small fleck of dark wood. 1½in. x 1⅞in. **7.** Beautifully turned English yew wood miniature salt from about 1780. 1½in. x 1½in.

Row 2.
1. Machine turned English rosewood salt from the late 19th century. 1in. x 2¼in. **2.** Red walnut miniature bowl found in Scotland. It has been particularly finely turned and dates from around 1800. It may be a salt but in view of its origin perhaps a whisky bowl was its more likely function. ⅞in. x 1in. **3.** English salt, probably from the North Country, made in oak and dating from the first quarter of the 19th century. 2in. x 1½in. **4.** English trencher salt in lignum vitae. In silver this design dates from 1705-20 but somehow this seems an over-optimistic date for this piece. 1in. x 3in. **5.** Small yew wood salt from about 1830 with a finely turned thin lip. 1½in. x 1½in. **6.** Finely turned English salt in cedar with the bowl supported with carved acanthus leaves. There are well-known examples of a similar form in silver in the Victoria and Albert Museum by Paul Crespin (1730) and Louis Cuny (1728) as well as the spool-shaped salts often made by Huguenot silversmiths between 1725-40. This treen salt, however, has unmistakable signs of 19th century origin, being machine turned and having beaded decoration on the lip. 1½in. x 2¼in.

Row 3.
1. Variegated rich patination on an English cedar salt from around 1860. 2in. x 1½in. **2.** English trencher salt, probably in fruitwood, with fabulous colour and patination from about 1770-90. 1¼in. x 2½in. **3 and 4.** Pair of English yew wood cups. They are probably salts but are 1½in. in depth with a square cut bottom to the bowl which contradicts this theory, though there is no obvious alternative. Good sheen and surface. c.1820. 3in. x 2¼in. **5.** A good English laburnum salt from around 1770-90. 1½in. x 2½in. **6.** A small English sycamore salt, 2⅜in. in height, shown in several groups of salts to give an impression of their comparative height.

Plate 7/14.

Row 1. 1. English fruitwood salt of about 1820. 2½in. x 2¼in. **2.** Horrible feeling English mahogany salt in perfect condition but of rather heavy design. In spite of the flattering lighting it has little character or charm. Late 19th century. 3¼in. x 3in. **3.** Very good English lignum vitae salt of about 1740 with an admirable flat foot and an elegant flare to the lip of the bowl as well as the fine 'craquelure' that tends to develop with age in lignum. 2½in. x 2¼in. **4.** English cedar salt with boring rather flat colour, c.1800. 2½in. x 2in. **5.** English fruitwood salt. The warmth and depth of colour in this piece contrasts with the uninteresting surface on its neighbour. It also has slight but attractive shrinkage across the grain – a beautiful tactile object. Last quarter of the 18th century. 2¼in. x 2⅜in. **6.** Small English bowl in lignum vitae which may be a salt. It is too small and light to be a wool bowl but could be a drinking vessel. This exemplifies one of the difficulties in attributing a function to a particular object. 1½in. x 1½in.

Row 2. 1. Solid uninteresting English walnut salt with no patination or glamour. c.1840. 2¼in. x 2⅜in. **2.** Intriguing object from Evan-Thomas Collection (label no.315) and illustrated in his book as a measure (plate 67). It is a beautifully turned object with a stepped inner surface to the bowl and made from a closely grained wood that is difficult to identify, though it could be box. It seems more likely to be a salt so is included here but its use must remain uncertain. Probably second half of 18th century. 3in. x 1⅞in. **3.** English red walnut salt c.1840. 3in. x 2½in. **4.** English salt, probably of laburnum, with an uncommonly long stem. c.1880. 3¼in. x 2½in. **5.** English fruitwood salt c.1800. 3¼in. x 2in. **6.** Rather squat English sycamore salt with quite a high domed foot and an unusually rich colour from some old varnish. 2½in. x 2in.

Row 3. 1. English yew wood salt of c.1750 with the warm coloration of the shell of a conker. 3in. x 2½in. **2.** English walnut salt with repaired foot. c.1800. 3¼in. x 3¼in. **3.** Provincial 18th century English ash salt with an interesting change in colour on the bowl at the level the salt would reach. 4⅛in. x 2½in. **4.** Particularly rich colour and patination for mahogany in an English salt of 1820-30. 3¼in. x 3½in. **5.** Small English sycamore salt 2⅜in. high shown in several groups of salts to give an impression of their variation in size.

Plate 7/15. The underside of three salts from the previous plate – no. 5 Row 2, no. 3 Row 2 and no. 3, Row 1, to show some of the differences in turning. **1 and 3** are pole lathe turned, the differences in the appearances being mainly related to the hardness of the wood. In **1** the chuck has been chiselled off, in **3** the central block has not been completely removed and this base shows good evidence of wear. **2** shows the screw hole for a large chuck. The base is flat having been sawn off. These features with the incised decoration are always late.

Plate 7/16. 1. A pretty little laburnum English salt of 1820 with particularly fine turning and pleasing colour. 1⅞in. x 2⅛in. **2.** English boxwood salt of early to mid-19th century with a notable high domed foot and good colour. 2¼in. x 2⅛in. **3.** English yew wood salt of eggcup form primitively turned with a square cut foot and rich glowing colour. This was previously in the Shepherd Collection (label no. 012 1649. Sotheby's sale 30.11.83, lot 757). c.1700. 2⅜in. x 2in. **4.** Unusual walnut urn-shaped probable salt with square base, a lovely faded colour and original patination. Mid-19th century. 3in. x 2in. **5.** Urn-shaped salt. The wood is a close grained fruitwood, possibly apple. The colour is rather sallow but with a lustrous surface. c.1850. 3in. x 2½in. **6.** Salt in very good coloured mahogany from the Sir Ambrose Heal Collection (Christie's sale 5.7.95, lot no.773). c.1840. 2½in. x 2⅜in.
Row 2. 1 and 6. A pair of English urn-shaped fruitwood salts c.1800. 2½in. x 2⅛in. **2 and 5.** A pair of English laburnum salts of Elizabethan shape but probably made around 1870. 2⅜in. x 2⅜in. **3 and 4.** A pair of heavily varnished sycamore salts giving them a poor colour, with artificial distressing to bases. c.1900. 1⅞in. x 2⅛in.
Row 3. 1. English salt from the first quarter of the 19th century. The wood has fine figuring and is possibly mulberry. 2½in. x 2½in. **2.** Pole lathe turned fruitwood salt with good base and wear as its main points of merit. Mid-18th century. **3.** Probably English North Country pole lathe turned sycamore salt with original but not very pleasing brown paint. Barrel shape to bowl and the high stem implies it is 19th century rather than a substantially earlier date which it is otherwise tempting to attribute. 3½in. x 2in. **4.** An English laburnum salt, second half 19th century. 3in. x 2½in. 5. English elm salt with a well defined foot. First quarter 19th century. 3in. x 2½in. **6.** Small English sycamore salt 2⅜in. high shown in several groups of salts to give an impression of the variation in size.

Plate 7/17. Row 1. 1. Rather ordinary English machine turned laburnum salt c.1850 with milling line decoration beneath the rim. The laburnum looks like polished stone. 2½in. x 3¼in. **2 and 5.** A pair of English mahogany salts being reasonable examples of their type c.1880. 3½in. x 2½in. **3 and 4.** A pair of rather uninteresting English beechwood salts with a good steeple base derived from an early style. Very late 19th century or early 20th century. 5in. x 2½in. **6.** An English salt of fruitwood, possibly cherry, c.1880. 3in. x 2½in.

Row 2. 1. English fruitwood salt c.1850. 2¼in. x 1½in. **2.** English mahogany salt c.1820. 2½in. x 2¼in. **3.** A boxwood possible salt c.1840-50. It is rather deep (1½in.) and has a square cut bottom making this use somewhat suspect. Nationality uncertain. 3¼in. x 2¼in. **4.** Rather ordinary English mahogany salt. Last quarter 19th century. 3½in. x 2½in. **5.** English walnut salt, well turned from a carefully chosen piece of wood. First quarter 19th century. 3in. x 2½in. **6.** English walnut salt. First quarter 19th century. 2½in. x 2¼in. **7.** English sycamore salt, c.1800, reputed to have originated in Somerset. 2½in. x 2⅜in.

Row 3. 1. English yew wood salt. First quarter 19th century. 1½in. x 1½in. **2.** English laburnum salt. This and the previous piece have square cut bottoms implying they might have had a different use. First quarter 19th century. 2⅛in. x 2¼in. **3.** Pretty standard English salt of African mahogany c.1830. The colour has the appearance of good quality Christmas pudding. 2½in. x 2½in. **4.** Unattractive English bleached laburnum salt c1880. 2¼in. x 2½in. **5.** Unexciting English laburnum salt, mid-19th century. 2½in. x 2½in. **6.** English oak salt made from the timbers of the *Royal George* which sank at Spithead in 1782. Timbers were recovered between 1836-40 by the Deane brothers and a Colonel Pasley and a small souvenir industry created numerous different articles of which this is an example. The entrepreneurs of the day. 1½in. x 1⅞in.

Row 4. 1. Six English sycamore salts and one of unidentified wood, all of very similar form but very differing colour, patination and therefore desirability. **5** may be the earliest (c.1800), the others being 19th century. **7** is the one used in previous plates to compare size and is 2⅜in. high.

Plate 7/18. 1. English lignum vitae salt with a domed and stepped foot and a short stem. c.1700. **2.** English oak salt with narrow disc turned decoration to the stem with a raised band round the lip and base and with incised line turned decoration between. Second quarter 19th century. **3.** English rosewood salt very similar in all its features to the larger example next to it. Rosewood was not in common usage before 1830. Second quarter 19th century. 2¼in. x 2in. **4.** English rosewood salt with reeded moulding to the bowl and foot and a vestigial knop on the short stem. Second quarter 19th century. 3½in. x 2½in. **5 and 7.** A pair of rich orange coloured boxwood salts. Mid-19th century. 3¼in. x 3in. **6.** English lignum vitae salt whose shape is reminiscent of a wassail bowl with three bands decorating the lower part of the bowl. Early 19th century. 2⅝in. x 2⅓in. **8.** English laburnum salt on a long stem with a strong everted roll-over rim. Late 19th century. 3¼in. x 2⅓in. **9.** English salt with a moulded foot. Late 19th century. 3¼in. x 2⅓in. **10.** Bold English lignum vitae cylindrical salt decorated with deeply incised bands. c.1800. 3½in. x 4½in. **11.** Small English sycamore salt, 2⅜in. in height, shown in several groups of salts to give an impression of their variation in size.

Plate 7/19. 1. Large English 19th century mahogany salt typical of rather heavy Victorian design, with a circular moulded foot, fussy decoration on the stem and overall a rather fat self-assured appearance. 5¼in. x 4¼in. **2.** Large English sycamore salt of completely uncertain date with rather odd gouged decoration to the base of the cup which is difficult to see in the picture. The skill of the photographer has hidden the 'wrinkles' on this lady who was probably begotten c.1925. 7½in. x 3½in. **3.** Sycamore salt of about 1800 with light coloured varnish in particularly good condition that has not acquired the grime of age. The shape of the foot suggests a Welsh origin. 4¼in. x 4¼in. **4.** Another large English 19th century mahogany salt to illustrate the diversity of shape and size of available salts. 5¼in. x 4¼in. **5.** English walnut salt from the early 19th century with quite pleasing patination and turning, a small knop, but not a piece to make the pulse race. 4¼in. x 2½in. **6.** English cedar salt of about 1840. 4in. x 3¼in. **7.** Small English sycamore salt, 2⅜in. in height, included in all group photographs as an indication of scale.

Plate 7/20. 1. An intriguing table salt made in the form of a wheelbarrow in solid yew wood though the legs have been replaced. This piece is made from specially selected timber and was possibly made to commission or as a gift to an enthusiastic gardener. While there are a few known silver examples this treen version is possibly unique. c.1760. 2in. x 1¼in. **2.** A standard English domestic footed table salt of barrel shape in solid yew. c.1800. 2½in. x 2in.

Plate 7/21. Very early English domestic spice pot, probably from the late 16th century, with excellent turning, great finial but rather unusual straight sides to the bowl. A rare and highly desirable survivor. 5½in. x 2½in.

Spice Pots and Containers

The use of spices in cookery goes back into the mists of time. In the Middle Ages they were regarded as necessities for their ability to help preserve food as well as to disguise the taste of meat that must sometimes have been exceedingly high if not actually bad. They were difficult to obtain, having to be brought from the Far East by caravan and ship to the merchants of Europe. The spice trade was of such importance that Holland, Spain, France and Portugal as well as Great Britain have been to war to establish control over it.

Early spice pots are very rare, may be ornamented with scratch decoration, are of varied shape and the attribution for their use is sometimes speculative. The decoration of the one illustrated in Plate 7/22 is characteristic of the late sixteenth century. The much commoner later ones dating from the late eighteenth through the nineteenth century are characterised by having a tower made up of from two to ten separate compartments that screw into each other. They were quite skilfully made by turners and some were produced in the Tunbridge Wells area (examples are on

Plate 7/22. English late 16th century spice pot with typical linear burned decoration. Sensational colour and underside with an old repair. 3½in. x 3½in.

view in the museum). Therefore some might be classified as 'Painted Tunbridge ware' and were produced over a limited period between 1780 and 1825.

When parquetry and mosaic work were introduced in about 1830 spice tower production dwindled. They all originally had paper labels and were varnished. Spice towers were made in various timbers and are of differing quality. Sycamore and beech are the most common with finer examples also found in fruitwood and occasionally box. Dating needless to say is complicated. There is a theory that suggests the overhang of the screw on the lids becomes more exaggerated as the lid itself takes a bolder and more domed form towards the last quarter of the nineteenth century. The earliest examples also tend to be found with

rather elaborate scroll decorated and shaped labels with hand-written calligraphic script to describe the contents of each section. As the nineteenth century progresses, these become fully printed labels, originally shaped and then developing into plain rectangular ones with rudimentary printed borders towards the end of the century.

One of the joys of collecting spice towers is that they can still be used for their original purpose without causing damage or eating tainted food, and they look particularly decorative in a kitchen. Condition is of crucial importance to a collector as many have split in an unsightly manner. Their appeal is more related to patination and colour than presumed date and a collection of towers with subtle differences in size, shape and style can be very attractive.

Plate 7/23. English lignum vitae spice jar from about 1700 with sensationally rich colour, very satisfying form and excellent turning marks. 8in. x 3½in.

Plate 7/24. Rare English spice jar and cover from about 1700, with wonderful patination and prominent pole lathe turning, particularly on the underside which also shows shrinkage and wear. 5¼in. x 3in.

Plate 7/25. 1. Maple mid-18th century bowl and cover probably used for spices. The old replacement of the finial in brass is not really in keeping with period. The bowl has been over cleaned but the colour inside is untouched. It could even be 'Baltic' rather than English. Not really sought after but included to show the spectrum of items presented to the collector developing his own judgement. 4¼in. x 3⅛in. **2.** Pole lathe turned English spice jar and cover in boxwood from the late 18th century. Excellent colour patination and wear. 4¼in. x 3½in. **3 and 5.** Pair of good English walnut spice jars with lids from the late 17th century. 5in. x 2½in. **4.** English walnut spice jar and cover from around 1770-80 with a good finial and fine patination. 5¼in. x 3in.

Plate 7/26. 1. Unusual burr box spice flask, certainly not English and possibly French. Patination is very modest. 6in. x 1½in. **2.** A much more imposing and grander version of the previous flask. The top with the ivory finial unscrews to reveal a container for a nutmeg or other spice. Unscrewing the remainder reveals the pierced top of the shaker. The nose doesn't reveal the original purpose of this wonderfully patinated object. They are clearly rare in this country. This one probably dates from the 18th century. Two comparable examples were sold at the Sotheby's 30.11.83 sale of the Shepherd Collection, lot 764. 8¼in. x 2in.

Plate 7/27. Four spice towers to show something of the variation in type. **1.** Extremely unusual lacquered four-tier spice tower with flower decoration. 5½in. x 3in. **2.** Six-tier spice tower. 11½in. x 3½in. **3.** Four-tier spice tower with replaced labels. 6½in. x 2½in. **4.** Three-tier spice tower with original paint and labels and a slightly higher domed lid. 6in. x 3⅛in.

Plate 7/28. English spice pot in laburnum from the second half of the 18th century. The picture shows the attractive rippled surface where the blade 'juddered' over the grain as sometimes happens with hard woods and/or blunt tools during turning.

Plate 7/29. Nutmeg grater and holder inspired by the Brighton Pavilion. This is the only nutmeg grater chosen to be illustrated because it is particularly, photogenic. A similar one is illustrated in *Tunbridgeware* (B. Austen) plate 6. c.1830. 5¼in. x 2½in.

CHAPTER 8

Mortars, Mortar Graters and Coffee Grinders

Plate 8/1. Giant English lignum vitae mortar which is 12in. high and 12½in. wide at the rim. The replacement pestle is clearly too small for this piece. The smaller mortar is shown for size comparison, 4⅛in. high (see Plate 8/2). c.1680.

In this chapter we shall look at three types of pulverising equipment. Metal and hardstone were, even from medieval times, the prime materials for mortars for obvious reasons. However large wooden mortars from this time, standing three feet high, are known made from a hollowed-out tree, usually oak or elm and sometimes with a stone or marble mortar inserted to provide the lower grinding surface.

Lignum vitae, because of its hardness and dense grain, became the wood of choice for mortars when importation started in the late sixteenth and early seventeenth centuries. Quite large examples survive, and one is illustrated,

Plate 8/2. 1. Very early, possibly c.1600, boxwood mortar with very fine turning and a well worn and patinated rim. Its nationality is uncertain, though possibly English. 4⅜in. x 2¾in. **2.** English lignum vitae mortar of fairly standard form but special because of the colour of the sap wood and its fine surface. Early 18th century. 4½in. x 3½in. **3.** Walnut bucket shaped (classical in brass) mortar with excellent colour and patination, possibly English. c.1700. 3¼in. x 2¾in.

but more commonly found are the smaller examples from the seventeenth and eighteenth centuries. Many base metal ones are dated so giving a useful precedent in helping to date treen examples.

The range of materials that needed to be pulverised or ground up is immense stretching from various foods to herbs, spices, sugar, tobacco, snuff, and coffee as well as medicines by the apothecary. There are thus three different types: the straightforward mortar and pestle, the mortar grinder in which two plates of metal with multiple jagged perforations are interposed to provide the grinding surfaces and finally the metal mechanical grinder housed within a wooden case, often made specifically for coffee.

Smaller pestle and mortars are made from many different woods, not predominantly lignum vitae. Their original exact purpose, whether apothecary, tobacco, snuff or for the kitchen, may be conjectural. However, shape is related to function and many smaller mortars are waisted to enable the user to get a good grip.

Plate 8/3. Very rare English 17th century lignum vitae mortar with original lid and pestle. This is similar, but very much smaller than one in the Pinto Collection in Birmingham (illustrated in fig.33 in his book). 4¾in. x 4¼in.

Plate 8/4. 1. An unusual mortar with an overhanging lid in lignum vitae with its pestle in a different wood – possibly sycamore. The presumption is that it is lidded to prevent spillage when grinding with liquid foods. Compare with the lidded mortar in Plate 8/3, and that from the Pinto Collection. 5½in. x 4½in. **2.** Cedar mortar with original pestle having interesting signs of wear round its middle where it has rubbed against the rim of the mortar. The body has a turned band, possibly to enhance the user's grip. The foot is unusually high. Mid-18th century. 5in. x 2in. **3.** Mortar and pestle found in Connecticut (USA) with a notably short stubby pestle. Made from an unidentified dense wood. 19th century. 6¼in. x 5in.

Plate 8/5 (Opposite). Particularly impressive English fruitwood mortar, inscribed 1669 which is probably correct. The base is oval in shape due to shrinkage in the solid and the pole lathe turning marks are notable. These features, together with its rich and varied chestnut colour, make this particularly collectable. 7½in. x 3½in.

Plate 8/5A (Above). The base, illustrating the shrinkage, turning marks and inscribed date.

Plate 8/6 (Left). Rare English late 17th century mortar with original hardwood pestle. While this is a standard early shape the deep honey lustrous colour makes it special. 6½in. x 3¾in.

Plate 8/7. These three objects are shown together because they have wonderful colour and patination and may all be mortars. **1 and 2** are finely turned, have rather everted rims, but seem insufficiently robust to be mortars, yet they have no other obvious use. They appear to be made from fruitwood c.1800. 5½in. x 2¾in. and 5in. x 2¾in. **3.** Clearly a mortar, made from sycamore. This tulip shape helps to date it to around 1830-40. 5in. x 2½in.

Plate 8/8. 1. English mid/late 18th century mortar, possibly of walnut, with original oak pestle, initialled CN on the base which has exceptional ribbed pole lathe turning. 4¼in. x 2¼in. **2.** English mid-18th century fruitwood (possibly cherry) snuff mortar with original pestle from the Sir Ambrose Heal Collection (Christie's lot 755, 5.7.95). Rich colour and patination. 5¼in. x 2¼in.

114

Plate 8/9. 1. English early 18th century fruitwood mortar with excellent colour and patination. 4¼in. x 2½in. Probably lot 467 Shepherd Collection sale. **2.** English mid-18th century beechwood mortar. 4½in. x 2½in. **3.** English mid-18th century fruitwood mortar with original pestle showing wear on the handle where it has rubbed on the edge of the mortar. This shape is fairly common but the base is finely turned. 3¾in. x 2½in. **4.** English early 18th century fruitwood mortar with pestle. 4½in. x 2½in.

Plate 8/10. 1. English mortar grinder missing pestle, c.1680. Fine turning, beautifully defined high domed foot. The bottom of the bowl and the under surface of the base show traces of pole lathe turning. The wood is rather dense and similar in colour to laburnum though it lacks any sapwood. The pattern of damage suggests the wood may be rather brittle. The difficulty in correctly attributing function is well illustrated by this piece. The bowl is 1½in. deep and square cut. Interestingly it was sold by a knowledgeable dealer as a salt and discussion with various experts, dealers and collectors failed to produce a better explanation. The mystery was solved when the second object was found, this time with its original pestle. The similarity between the two pieces is uncanny and makes correct identification of the function of the first obvious. 6in. x 2¾in. **2.** English mortar grinder with original pestle c.1680 with similar wood, turning and base. The quality of the design of this piece is not quite as excellent as the first. It may be that this is of slightly later date, the foot being not quite so elegantly designed. The notable bold ball finial serves as a handle. The heavy dense timber and large finial imply that some pressure was required for grinding whatever these pieces were designed for. 10½in. x 3⅛in.

Plate 8/11. Remarkable pole lathe turned English mortar c.1660 in fruitwood with striking reeded decoration to the body and foot. This was previously in the Evan-Thomas Collection and illustrated in his book, plate 26. 7in. x 3½in.

Plate 8/12. This English 'gun barrel' shaped mortar grinder is of a very rare type dating from around 1680. This form is typical of the late 17th century, being seen in the leg turning of joined stools and table legs at this period, terminating in a foot with a classical baroque moulding. The wood is probably yew. 6¾in. x 2½in.

Plate 8/13. 1. A fine large English sycamore mortar grater with excellent rich nutty colour and patination and a deeply concave turning to the underside of the foot now partly replaced. Last quarter 17th century. 10½in. x 3¾in. **2.** Small, modestly patinated sycamore mortar grater, probably English, with traces of painted red band decoration. First half 18th century. **3.** English sycamore mortar grater with a good concave underside, though with slight damage to the rim. Last quarter of the 17th century. 10in. x 3¼in.

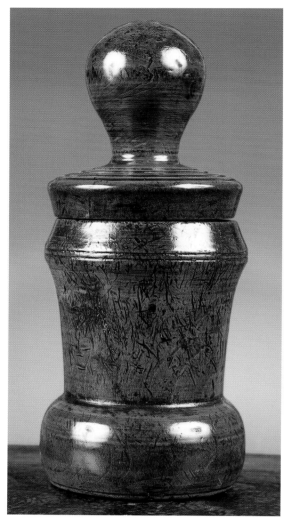

Plate 8/14 (Above). This English sycamore mortar grinder from the first half of the 18th century has an appealing honey coloured patination as well as a very pleasing form. 8⅜in. x 3¼in.

Plate 8/15 (Above right). 1. English mortar grater, c.1680, with regular bands of ring turned decoration, an old stapled repair and five dots that need to be aligned to remove the base, much in the style of a modern child-proof medicine bottle. The pestle doesn't fit snuggly, as can be seen, but this is probably due to old damage. There are very faint traces of polychrome decoration. 9¼in. x 4in. **2.** A simple domestic sycamore mortar grater from the first half of the 19th century patinated with grease from the kitchen. 6¾in. x 3in.

Plate 8/16 (Right). 1. Fine English lignum vitae bullet shaped coffee grinder with bold original acorn finial which unscrews to reveal the turning mechanism. Late 18th century. This piece has some minor chips, but is otherwise undamaged with a lovely colour. 8¼in. x 2¼in. **2.** Very rare early English lignum vitae coffee grinder of lighthouse shape, c.1720. The upper and lower sections have turned moulded rims with carved beaded decoration. Each of the three sections has an interesting stylised bead and dot decoration and the flared foot has broad, boldly carved detail. 9in. x 3¼in.

Plate 8/18. English lignum vitae coffee grinder with traces (as occasionally found in early pieces of treen made from lignum vitae) of an opaque golden/bronze coloured surface film, now rather broken up (see Plate 19/7) but with evident signs of craquelure and age. c.1760. 7½in. x 4¼in.

Plate 8/17. English bullet shaped coffee grinder showing the contrasting colours in lignum vitae with a short stem and rounded foot. c.1830. 10in. x 3¼in.

CHAPTER 9

Spoons, Ladles and Love Spoons

Plate 9/1. A selection of small spoons dating from 1720. The fourth, with a turned knop, is of pear wood and has a particularly attractive milky patination. Two with tapering upturned ends have a shape reminiscent of Caernarvon spoons. The one with the flattened handle, presumably taking its inspiration from silver forms, has charmingly self-important initials AS and some chip carving to its end; probably from 1720. The one on the extreme right is probably for a child and has teeth marks on the end of the handle.

The variety of woods, styles, functions, colours, and shapes of wooden spoons and ladles is enormous and again the differences in their design relate to their purpose. The basic cooking, stirring and eating spoons are still made and used today, having changed little, and are largely undatable. Every housewife has her favourite spoon in the kitchen. But even at this rather mundane level a collection concentrating on one special aspect, such as the way they were used, the variety of shapes, forms, and patination, can have considerable interest, be very decorative and not necessarily burst the budget.

Representative examples of various groups under these headings are illustrated to show something of their differences. These will include ladles, Welsh cawl and different handed spoons, more ordinary kitchen and eating spoons and, because of their intrinsic interest, some Welsh love spoons, even though they weren't really intended to be used.

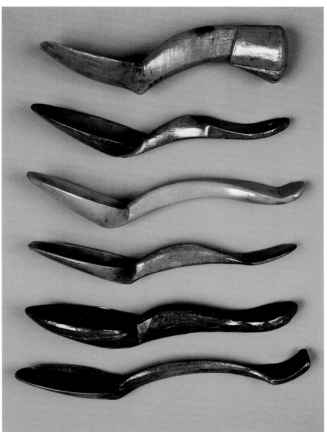

Plates 9/2 and 9/3. A selection of Welsh spoons, seven pictured from above and six from the side. These dolphin shaped spoons with an upturn of the end of the handle and the rather odd deepening of the central part are said to be typical of Caernarvonshire. The spoon one from the bottom is unusual, being of bog oak. The second one down (or top right) seems to have a handle that duplicates as a pestle. They are all very pleasing and easy to hold so it is not clear why these designs haven't become generally popular.

Plate 9/4. A collection of uncommon and attractively quaint Welsh spoons made for right- or left-handed use. The four on the left are right-handed, the rarer one on the right being the only left-handed example. These are commonly regarded as Welsh but are not now found specifically emerging from Wales. Again they are very comfortable to use.

Plate 9/5. Two views of a glorious chip-carved and rat tailed Welsh spoon c.1780. 4⅛in. x 1in.

Plate 9/6. Fourteen Welsh cawl spoons in various woods, many having the rather characteristic oval shape to the bowl and two with turned finials to the ends of the handles. These spoons show tremendous variation in colour and surface and can make a very satisfying collection on their own. Probably 19th and early 20th century.

Plate 9/7. Five Welsh spoons. The three on the right are cawl spoons showing various styles of handle decoration. That on the left is clearly derived from the love spoon tradition. 19th century.

Plate 9/8. Three Welsh spoons with flat section ends to their handles derived from the trifid form in silver. The original decorative carving to the face of the centre spoon is of a considerably earlier date than 1800 inscribed on its back. This spoon and the one inscribed AS probably date from first quarter of the 18th century.

Plate 9/8A (Far right). The back of the centre spoon in Plate 9/8.

Plate 9/9. A small collection of five condiment spoons, one being particularly long (10in.) and the only one made from sycamore, the others being box. 4⅛in. long.

Plate 9/10. In the centre are an unusual matching spoon and fork in boxwood that were probably presentation pieces. On either side are a separate 'working' spoon and fork (not a pair), also in boxwood. Third quarter of 19th century.

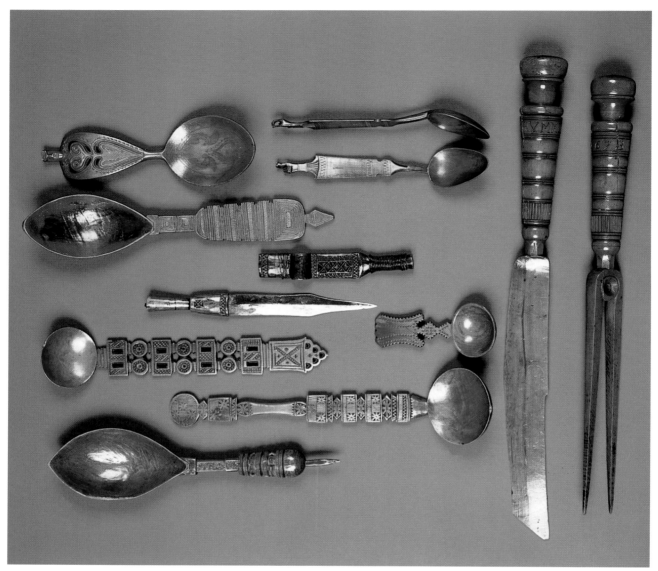

Plate 9/11. A miscellaneous collection of various spoons, a knife and a presentation knife and fork. These are in fruitwood, are inscribed 'ANNO1673' on the fork and 'RUMMELIACOBUS' on the knife. Their significance and nationality await further study. The chip-carved knife with its sheath in the centre is not Welsh but African. The small chip-carved caddy spoon is Welsh and rather unusual in wood. Otherwise these spoons form a collection of oddities. Chip carving was common to many other countries beyond Europe and the shape of the bowls of some of these implies a non-European origin. The spoon (bottom left) with the intricately carved decoration to the handle carries the Evan-Thomas Collection label 313.

Love Spoons

Plate 9/12 (Opposite). Left, a large personal and elaborate Welsh love spoon in beech with four integrally carved spoons issuing from a rectangular panel pierced with stylised rosettes and other motifs with two quiver finials and a particularly warm variegated colour. Early 19th century. Previously in A.T. Collection 240. 18½in. x 6½in. Right, another particularly large Welsh fruitwood love spoon with a chip-carved monogram and pierced decoration. Early 19th century. 20in. long.

Plate 9/13 (Opposite). A collection of nine love spoons of varying complexity. The central three have all been made in workshops as evidenced by very similar examples known and exhibited. The pale sycamore spoon (top left), with stylised floral pierced decoration to the flattened handle, is of a school producing high quality but relatively simple spoons that could have actually been used. Next to it this love spoon of remarkable finesse and craftsmanship is made from a single piece of wood – the chain and balls included. The design is comparable to that seen in Pinto plate 161 D&C, a Sotheby's auction of 1984, an anonymous sale at Phillips (10.9.93, lot 486) and National Museum of Wales examples numbers 45, 46, and 47.

The central spoon with rectangular panel pierced with hearts and other decoration, including the initials ME and the date 1836, forms part of a group of spoons of similar concept and date, though an exact replica has not been found. To the right of this the fruitwood love spoon dated 1849 is clearly from the same workshop as those illustrated in Sotheby's Shepherd Collection sale of 30/11/83 lot 678, Evan-Thomas plate 57h and National Museum of Wales No 1059 amongst others. The deep nutty brown love spoon with four pierced hearts (top right) is also in sycamore but with a different finish from the previous one. It is of late 18th century origin and has a hugely satisfying combination of patina and form.

The spoon (bottom left) with pierced hearts decorating the flattened handle as well as a letter box also has chip-carved decoration and is initialled L on the back. The bowl has been reduced making it look rather stumpy. Last quarter 18th century. The rather similar spoon (bottom right) again has pierced heart decoration to the handle but this is more complex with a 'U' shaped hoop behind connecting the two sides of the handle and another connecting this to the base of the bowl. c.1800. Both these last two spoons seem likely to have been personally and not workshop made.

The top horizontal spoon has the high shape of a Caernarvon spoon but with chip carving and a pierced heart as decoration. This is another example of a simple but very attractive piece developing from the love spoon tradition. First quarter 19th century. The spoon lying horizontally at the very bottom is shown face down as it has an unexpected trapped ball behind the handle as well as the initials 'TH' and the date 1836. The front of the handle is chip-carved with additional incised heart decoration. It represents the spirit of folk art – simple naïvity and unpretentiousness.

Plate 9/14. English fruitwood ladle, the bowl and handle being turned separately. This has two knops and a disc to prevent the ladle falling into the punch bowl and for ease in ladling. c.1690. The almost exact replica in the Victoria and Albert Museum is not in such pristine condition. 12½in. long.

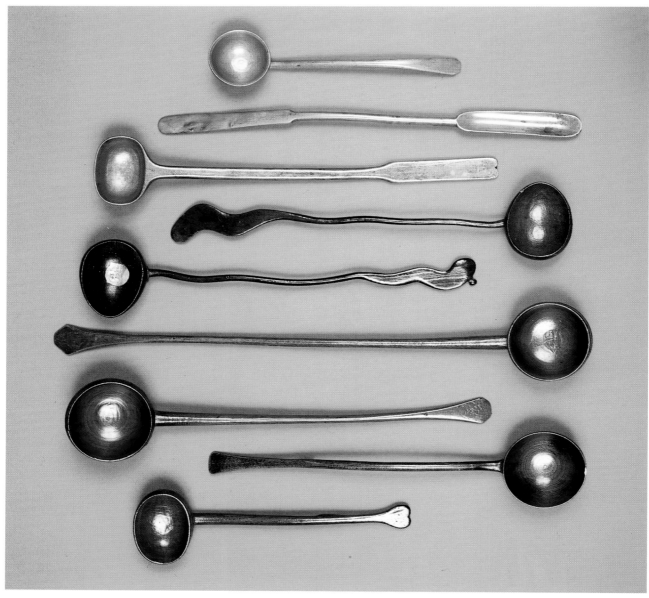

Plate 9/15. A collection of eight English punch ladles and a single boxwood marrow scoop. This is very rare in wood but follows the design of the much commoner ones in silver. The ladles vary in length from 7¾in. to 16in. long and are in sycamore, box and fruitwoods. The two with wiggly handles clearly come from the same maker, their only difference being the small knob finial on the end of the handle of the one from the Evan-Thomas Collection (numbered (2) 890), and illustrated in his book, plate 48. The second never had this feature and was not part of the original pair shown in his book. The handle of the one with the oval bowl extends from its rim rather than the side, both features being rather unusual.

Plate 9/16. Huge, extensively chip-carved sycamore 'Love' basting spoon. Similar examples are known with late 17th and 18th century dates, names and sometimes mottoes incorporated within the carved decoration and are believed to have formed part of the Welsh love spoon tradition. Sadly this one has only geometric chip-carved motifs and no inscriptions. Origin uncertain. Early 19th century. 20in. long.

Plate 9/17. 1. A particularly elegant Welsh sycamore ladle from the last quarter of the 18th century with a remarkable sheen, particularly under the handle, from years of natural polishing in use. It also has an incised floral motif to the handle which adds further interest. Approximately 6in. across. **2.** Welsh sycamore ladle with evidence of considerable use – the underside of the handle again being highly polished. The handle is decorated with incised and carved stylised flowers. The profile shape again has particular elegance. This was probably dairy associated. c.1820. 6¾in. across. **3.** Welsh fruitwood ladle, clearly much younger and clumsier than the other examples but showing residual memory of a previous generation of more sophisticated carvers. Some floral carved decoration to the handle. Probably made this century. 6¼in. across. **4.** A beech ladle with probably a pseudo coat of arms and a carved heart on the handle and a transverse bowl. These features make it likely to be Scandinavian and it should not be confused with the Welsh ones. Previously in the Evan-Thomas Collection, label no. 271 and illustrated in his book, plate 46a. 18th century. 7in. across.

Plate 9/17A. Sideways view of the ladles in Plate 9/17 to show the elegance of their design in profile.

Plate 9/18. 1. Sycamore ladle with well worn old paint used, from the pattern of the wear and patination, mainly by a right-handed man. It was acquired from an antique market in Milan so is unlikely to be Welsh which would otherwise have been one's guess as to provenance. A lovely and very simple object inscribed with the initials I:O. 19th century. 10½in. long. **2.** Worn, dilapidated and abandoned old scoop now loved again because of its wizened appearance, tatty edge and old repairs with string and wire. Age and nationality irrelevant but a charming old thing. 8in. across handle.

Plate 9/19. 1. Beech scoop, probably Welsh from second half 19th century, that happens to be well shrunk across the grain. 1¾in. x 6¾in. (including handle). **2.** Late 18th century sycamore ale scoop of typical size and shape. 2¼in. x 9in. **3.** Sycamore scoop, probably for cream, but included here because of the interest in the turning. Initially the turner made the rather pleasing upturned flange in a complete circle and only then cut away ⁹⁄₁₀ of the ring to leave the residual flange as an elegant handle. He clearly started with a large piece of wood as similarly required for the negus strainers (see Plate 15/10, 3). c.1800.

Plate 9/20. A collection of ladles and a spoon. The heart motif on the nearest one probably indicates it was a love spoon given to a wife who was expected to do a bit of work and hefty ladling. The smaller sycamore one is really quite elegant with the curves of its hook.

Plate 9/21. 1. A beech grain scoop in an excellent state of preservation and dating from mid–19th century. 1½in. long. **2.** An English sycamore pap boat, early 19th century. A single example of these is shown. They come in many shapes, sizes and materials and were widely used for feeding infants and invalids. Extensively carved ones are usually Continental.

CHAPTER 10

Roundels

Plates 10/1 and 10/2. Two views of a typical though very rare English roundel case containing ten plain roundels (not shown) without decoration. These show the incised decoration with arrows and cross-hatching as well as the ancient stapled repair. The decoration is entirely characteristic, dating this piece to around 1570. 6½in. x 2½in.

A very authoritative account of roundels was given by Professor A.H. Church, FRS in 1894. Thirty or forty sets were known to him, many of which were already in museums.

They are painted tablets of wood, usually circular, 5in. to 6in. in diameter but only 1/16in. to 1/8in. thick, made from sycamore or beech and contained in a circular carved box. These were made from the fifteenth to the sixteenth century and are extremely rare.

There are two partially conflicting ideas on their original use. There is good documentary evidence that banquets in Elizabethan and Stuart times may have ended with the serving of fruits, sweetmeats, marzipan, cheese and other confections. It is usually taken that they were served on roundels or fruit trenchers used with the plain side uppermost. The roundel would then be turned over revealing the delicate painted decoration, often with Elizabethan motifs, and one or two carefully inscribed

verse rhymes on a very wide variety of subjects. These were then recited or sung by members of the company.

The alternative idea is that they were a sort of after-dinner pastime, each guest drawing one and reciting or singing the short epigrams or 'Poesies' as they were called. The subjects of the verses include satirical poems, moralising stories and biblical quotations. Henry Ellis in 1852 quotes from a book of 1611 that includes the musical composition for verses from a roundel for 'Violl de Gambo, the lute, and the Voyce to sing the verse…'

Plate 10/3. Sensational rich patination on a plain English roundel case in sycamore decorated only with incised rings. This may be a little later – slightly after 1600. It contains five painted roundels, three exactly fitting the case and presumably original to it and two slightly smaller that stylistically are earlier in date. See Plates 10/6 to 10/8. 6in. x 2½in.

Plates 10/4 and 10/5.

The two earlier roundels with painting and scrolling entirely typical of Elizabethan decoration. The writing translates as follows:

10/4.

Learn before thou/speake	Eccl. 18.
Talke wysely and/honestly	Eccl. 22.
Abyde by thye worde	Eccl. 5.
Be not hasty in thy/tonge	Eccl. 4.

The main evidence against their being eaten off is that they usually are not scarred with knife marks, not stained or patinated in the way trenchers are and show no other signs of wear. Further, the paintings appear to be too delicate to survive washing up even though coated with a tough varnish on the painted side. Even the completely unadorned set from the box illustrated in Plates 10/1 and 10/2 which are not varnished show no signs of use or wear, but presumably served some purpose. A further similar set seen in the Victoria and Albert Museum again showed no signs of use. Examination of half a dozen painted sets in the museum revealed the same pattern – no wear on the plain side and no damage to the varnished and painted side. This evidence makes it very difficult to accept that the ones examined could have seen much use in contact with juicy fruit or sticky confections.

Many known sets are incomplete but it seems unlikely that this was because the missing ones were thrown away worn out from use yet with the remaining ones being perfectly preserved.

Some of the roundel boxes seem rather similar with the Royal Coat of arms flanked by the initials 'ER'. Pinto suggests that these may have been gifts from the Queen to members of the nobility who had given her costly New Year presents, as was the custom.

However they were actually used in their time, they remain rare and precious objects which should give us insight into life in the first Elizabethan age.

Five painted roundels have been fully illustrated here almost life size to show their detail and finesse. The 'Poesies' are in rather quaint old English and have kindly been translated by Peter Brears.

10/5.
Wedlocke ye to/be…e/ in honour/amonge/all men/and the bedde/undefyled
As for whore/kepers/and ad= /ueaters/God shall /Judge/them.
My sonne kepe thee well from all/whordom, and besydes thy wyfe/
see that no fau(l)te be knowen/of thee   Tob.

Plates 10/6–10/8. These are the three that fit the box and presumably are part of the original set.

10/6.
Content ty selfe/w(i)th thynne estatt/
And sende noo poore/wight from thy gatt/
For wi(th)e this councell I thye geve
To learne to die and die to Iyve

10/7.
Thy fortuine/is full longe to Iyve/
For nature dothe longe/lyfethe(e) geve
But once a weke thou wilte/be sicke
And have a sullen agewes/fytt
[Ague is a periodic swinging fever.]

10/8.
Though hongrie/mele be put in pott/Yett conscence cleare kept wythe out spott/
Doth kepe thye corpes in quiet rest/Then he that/thousandes hathe in a cheste

CHAPTER 11

Platters, Trenchers, Bowls and Dishes

In the fifteenth and sixteenth centuries bread was baked in the form of thick flat discs which was served fresh to the lord of the manor and high ranking guests, others having it one day old. Square trenchers were cut from bread up to four days old and used by all the company, though square wooden trenchers were also used. The custom of throwing trenchers to the dogs becomes comprehensible when one realises these were old bread, by the end of the meal soaked in whatever was being eaten. In the seventeenth century food was brought to the table in large wooden bowls, individuals helping themselves with spoons or fingers on to their bread or wooden trencher. Trenchers with a turned central depression were obviously found to be more practical in retaining the juices than flat ones and these often had a small turned cavity in one corner for salt. Cutting off the corners led to the development of round trenchers which then became known as platters, though the terms are really synonymous.

Pewter began to replace wooden trenchers by the mid to later part of the seventeenth century and silver and pottery became increasingly commonplace, depending on circumstances. By the early eighteenth century porcelain and finer ceramics were used by the wealthy, but wooden examples continued to be used into the twentieth century. The wood selected was usually sycamore or beech, the former responding particularly well to repeated scraping and scrubbing as it didn't splinter, roughen up the grain or transmit its taste. Beech can lend a slightly bitter taste.

Trenchers and platters were not costly items and most must have been thrown away when broken or very worn – an early manifestation of the 'disposable society'. Thus early trenchers are extremely rare and so have become very expensive. They are very simply made objects and there are numerous 'forgeries'. Trenchers and platters are supremely difficult to date. Their form is usually simple, the wear is very variable depending on usage, their style didn't alter radically over centuries and initialling or marking, whether by the maker or owner, is unusual. When trying to assess the wear and surface of an old platter the things to look for are randomness in the knife marks, which should have signs of variable age (these judged by their differing 'sharpness'), wear on both sides and discoloration. You must look particularly for intentional distressing. The best attempt to distil some guidance for collectors interested in platters is the article by Peter Hornsby (see Appendix V). In conclusion, dating platters accurately is complicated even for experts and purchases should be made on grounds of feel and personal response to the object.

It is an area of the market where prices are within a reasonable range as long as you aren't aiming to make a big collection of genuinely early square trenchers with salt cavities.

The location of bowls dishes and plates (as defined by the Trust) found in the *Mary Rose* which sank in 1545 is very interesting in relation to the use of drinking vessels and plates. There were relatively few plates but the dishes were presumably used for eating. Of 116 dishes recovered (height less than one-third but greater than one-seventh of its diameter), 110 were beech. Ninety-two were found near the galley, many being in barrels. A few were stamped with 'H' implying they may have been an issue to the ship by the authorities and their location by the galley contrasts with the distribution of bowls.

In contrast no goblets were found anywhere and altogether less than fifty drinking vessels in any material were retrieved. There were some stave built tankards and larger vessels, but there was no uniformity in their size, number of staves or wood. There was some concentration in their location to areas close to the galley and by the carpenter's cabin. The fascinating thing is that the fifty-six small bowls were found in all parts of the ship and not concentrated round the galley. These were made from a wide variety of woods and often decorated with initials and graffiti. A possible and intriguing interpretation of

Plate 11/1 (Opposite). This remarkable shallow dish or platter has great surface markings and patination 'to die for', the collector's dream! A close-up is shown in Chapter 19 (Plate 19/21). This survivor is initialled on the base and is very similar to designs recovered from the wreck of the *Mary Rose,* but it probably dates from c.1700. 2¾in. x 11in. in diameter.

Three pictures published by kind permission of the Mary Rose Trust to illustrate in particular the form of some of the bowls found in this wreck which sank in 1545. The small one with the two spoons is very similar to those shown in Plates 11/1, 11/13 and 11/25. The one next to it has a bevelled outside rim, a feature often regarded as North Country or Scottish in origin. Note especially the individual initials and markings found on some bowls. Also note the pepper-mill, the tankard and the staved flagon. The importance of these examples is the insight they shed on the common utensils of the period.

these findings is that these bowls were personal belongings rather than being communal and were probably used for both drinking and eating.

The exact function of the various bowls available to collectors, whether feeding, drinking, dairy or for some other purpose is still an area of speculation. The *Mary Rose* information gives licence to informed speculation. The illustration of bowls here has been limited by trying to exclude those more likely to have been used in the dairy while at the same time showing a range of sizes, shapes and woods, hoping to entice others to form collections and maybe shed light on specific function.

Plate 11/2 (Opposite above). A collection of square platters with separately turned salt cavities from Hampton Court Palace. It is interesting to note the picture (dated 1793) reproduced in *English Vernacular Furniture* by Christopher Gilbert (plate 49) of a 'Cottage interior with an old woman preparing tea' by W.R. Bigg (now in the Victoria and Albert Museum) which illustrates a stack of square platters on a shelf as well as a round one on a tripod table. Crown copyright: Historic Royal Palaces

Plate 11/3 (Opposite). Two square English beech platters, the smaller with a circular depression for salt. Because they are rare and highly prized, fakes have been made which can be difficult to distinguish from the genuine early examples. These two look 'right' in that they have appropriate wear on both sides, are quite slim, seem to have a coating of old bone varnish and have the right 'feel' to make it believable that they were made in 1700 or earlier. ½in. x 6¾in. square and ½in. x 7¾in. square.

Plate 11/4. A particularly charming twisted and warped English sycamore platter branded with the initials F.D. twice to the underside. This shows remarkable contortion without any splitting and has extensive signs of wear and usage both in the bowl and on the base. Mid-18th century. 1in. x 8½in at the rim.

Plate 11/5. 1. A rich nutty sycamore platter with a reeded rim and of slightly sturdier construction. The back is branded with an inscription reading 'T JONES' & 'BLACKMORE'. c.1800. ⅞in. x 8¾in. **2.** A good honest English sycamore platter with appropriate signs of wear. c.1800. ½in. x 10in.

Plate 11/5A. The backs of two of the platters shown in previous plates (11/4 and 11/5) to show the wear and the branded inscriptions.

Plate 11/6. English sycamore platter of the 18th century with wonderful patination, decades of knife cuts and aeons of poor washing up without a dishwasher – in other words a surface greatly prized by the collector. ⅞in. x 8½in.

Plate 11/7. Dramatically pockmarked and petrified looking English sycamore platter with genuine patina of variegated russet hues. Last quarter 18th century. 1⅛in. x 8¾in.

Plate 11/8. English sycamore platter of rather poor colour and not much attraction but of obvious age with marked shrinkage across the grain. Possibly North Country and c.1770. Old museum mark. From Pitt Rivers Collection. 1⅛in. x 7½in.

Plate 11/9. A sycamore platter with a steeply raised rim which is illustrated particularly to show the result of normal wear that has thinned its centre from about ½in. to wafer thinness with two holes, thus destroying its useful life. It must have been much loved to have survived for us to enjoy now. c.1800. 1¼in. x 8¼in.

Plate 11/10. 1. English sycamore platter with unusual and interesting footed base with concave underside, c.1800. Clearly it was designed for a particular purpose which now must be speculative. As platters at this time were used on both sides perhaps it was used for more liquid food or pottage. It is however an unusual design and possibly originated from the North Country. 1⅜in. x 5⅜in. **2.** English beechwood platter with excellent patination, a thin rim and a small foot dated to the second half of the 18th century. There is little wear on the base so it was not used extensively as a bowl, which contrasts with the possible double purpose of the previous example. This was previously in the Evan-Thomas Collection and retains his label, no. 623. Subsequently it was in the Shepherd Collection sale at Sotheby's, lot 252. 1¼in. x 7½in.

Plate 11/10A. Backs of the platters.

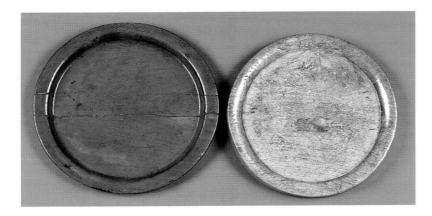

Plate 11/11. 1. English sycamore platter with modest rim and old break bearing the labels from the Evan-Thomas (no. 807) and Shepherd Collections (KD1450) and possibly dating from the late 18th century. This does not appear in the Sotheby's sale catalogue so presumably must have been sold at a different time. ⅜in. x 8¾in. **2.** English sycamore platter with similar rim, good evidence of wear and inscribed WF on the base, from the late 18th century. Previously in the DL Collection. ⅜in. x 8¼in.

Plate 11/11A. Backs of the platters shown above.

Plate 11/12. A group of nine platters including two pairs to illustrate the diversity in form. The two small rimmed sycamore platters in the front were from Sir Ambrose Heal's Collection (lot 778, Christie's 5.7.95) having a prominent concave foot and moderately deep bowl. One is 5½in. and the other 6in. in diameter. Second quarter 19th century. The second pair in the front row are in sycamore with single reeded decoration on the narrower rim, mid-19th century. The knife marks on the front resonate with their genuine extensive use. 8¼in. in diameter.
Second row. First on the left is a possibly mid-19th century platter, 9in. in diameter, with a flat bottom and a narrow sunken rim, probably in sycamore. The distressing (shown in close-up in Plate 18/4) looks artificial. The next is a sycamore platter initialled RG, with a good skin, genuine wear back and front and a simple raised rim curving into the base. Second half 18th century. 10in. in diameter. The third in this row is of similar form to the last, also in sycamore but with a broader rim. The colour appears to be stained and it lacks sincerity and depth. Mid-19th century. 9½in. in diameter.
Back row. Left is a modest sycamore platter with a cushioned rim, mid-19th century. 8in. in diameter. Right is a Wentworth platter from the Darton Collection, initialled EWF. It has a flat bottom, a well defined cushioned rim and an appealing richly varying colour. Early 19th century. 8¾in. in diameter.

Plate 11/13. 1. Small bowl with carved initials IG. The underside is applied with a hand-inscribed paper label 'SMALL BASIN or BOWL – fruit-wood carved on the side IG 1½" high-4⅛" wide English: 16 or 17th. cent:, from Evan-Thomas coll'. This appears to be sycamore and probably not earlier than the 17th century. The inside of the bowl has remarkable wear, colour and patination (see Plate 11/25). **2.** This mid-18th century sycamore platter of particularly rare small size and perfect proportions shows evidence of much use and must have had a specific purpose, possibly for fine delicacies such as sweetmeats or made for a child. Ex-Shepherd Collection. c.1750. 5¼in. in diameter.

Plate 11/14. 1. A large circular English elm serving or carving board, known as 'common dish', with incised ring turned border and slightly raised rim, originating from Dartmoor. c.1740. 1in. x 14¾in. **2.** A large circular sycamore platter with a slightly raised rim and showing a lustrous pale patination. c.1800 1in. x 15in.

Plate 11/15. A solid walnut square platter with all round moulded gravy or juice channel, having a raised turned circular foot to the underside. This could be English. c.1780. 1in. thick x 10¾in. square.

Plate 11/15A. Underside of Plate 11/15.

Plate 11/16. A massive English sycamore rectangular serving platter, sometimes known as 'the common dish', measuring 24in. x 17in. The deep central recess suggests it was made for serving joints of meat and that the steep moulded rim retained the juices. Mid-18th century. It is shown with a bowl and platter to emphasise its size.

Plate 11/17. At the back is a large sycamore platter 20in. in diameter with a freshly washed look and with a relatively thin rim. It is raised to just over 1in. on a convex base. First half 19th century. On the left is a large sycamore dish with remarkable variation in the depth of colour and patination. 3⅛in. x 18in. at the rim. c.1770. On the extreme left is a rare large beech strainer, 2¾in. x 12in. in diameter. Its crusty old brown surface colour has been worn away in places, particularly on the base, to reveal the polished wood beneath. 18th century. On the right is a sycamore platter raised on a small foot with a shallow raised rim. The whole shows wear and battering from use and overall is rather contorted, making it an interesting and particularly collectable piece. Mid-18th century. 17in. in diameter. On the extreme right is a shallow possibly American butternut wood bowl with a particularly rich dark honeyed colour. First quarter 19th century. 14½in. across the bowl and 3in. high. In the front is the small Evan-Thomas bowl (Plate 11/13, 1) for purpose of scale.

Plate 11/18. A bowl notable for its curly warping and because, unusually, it is in ash. c.1780. 2½in. x 10¾in. at the rim.

Plate 11/19. Three English bowls. The sturdy elm one on the left with the residue of its original paint has become rather oval in shape. It has four bands of incised decoration to the bowl. A rugged probably North Country feeding bowl. 3½in. x 7¼in. at the rim. Early 19th century. Elm 'log' bowl c.1800 with a solid ¾in. foot, the whole cut across the grain from a log. This design is quite well known in two sizes, this and a smaller one, and they must have been made in reasonable numbers to turn up in the way they do. Pinto suggests these are eating bowls which all came from the same Sussex farmhouse, being made there in this unusual way over many years. This view is not completely accepted, some believing they are till bowls for money or salts. This example has no particular signs of a specific use. My belief is that they were made as farmhouse eating bowls and produced over a long period of time. Some examples date from the mid-18th century or earlier and others of this same form date comfortably from the 19th century. 7in. x 3¼in. The small bowl in the front (Plate 11/13, 1) is shown again to give an impression of their comparative sizes.

Plate 11/20. Four English bowls. The pale scoop at the back has a very fine varnished surface which is sufficiently transparent to allow the grain to be seen. through it, thus giving it the appearance of having an almost milky skin except at the rim where the wood is more visible. It is widely accepted that this milky appearance, seen mainly in objects used in the dairy, is the result of repeated exposure to and absorption of casein from the milk. Almost certainly for use in the dairy but included here because of its particularly attractive appearance that contrasts with the surfaces on the other bowls. Early 19th century. 1¾in. x 7in. at the rim. On the left is a small bowl for eating and or drinking. It is pleasingly oval in shape, chestnut brown in colour and made from elm. 19th century. 2⅓in. x 5¼in. at the rim. On the right is a slightly oval small fruitwood bowl with an inverted rim. It is finely turned with twin lines of incised decoration on the rim, on the outside of the bowl and to the inside of its bottom. Last quarter 18th century. Its colour is a rich nutty brown. It could have been used for either eating, drinking or both. 1¾in. x 5¼in. at the rim. In the front the small Evan-Thomas bowl is shown again for size and colour comparisons to be made.

Plate 11/21. Two medium sized sycamore bowls of similar design and decoration to that in the previous illustration. Very good turning. This form may possibly be Scottish. These again have a very rich colour. 1780–1820. 3in. x 8in. at the rim and 2½in. x 7in. The small bowl is again shown for comparative purposes.

Plate 11/22. A pair of small bowls, probably in sycamore though it is difficult to be sure as they have been stained a rather unpleasant slightly sickly uniform brown colour difficult to read through. Interestingly, they have the same inverted rim to their design as previously discussed, but overall these are cruder in design, the quality of their turning and their finish. Their merit is in the inscription on the base of both of them which reads 'B.W.Jackson Architect Halifax … [unreadable] 1870'. 2in. x 5½in.

Plate 11/23. Four bowls. Two shallow English sycamore bowls (left and right) usually regarded as dairy, especially if they exhibit the pale lustrous patination seen on these which is attributed to repeated contact with casein in milk. c.1800. Both 2¾in. x 11in. at the rim.

At the back a distinctive bowl in a very dense hardwood reminiscent of lignum vitae with craquelure and shrinkage across the grain implying turning before extensive seasoning. But it has a rather wide grain and is without the characteristic odour of this wood so presumably is from a different imported hardwood. Date uncertain but could be 19th century. 3¼in. x 11in. at the rim.

The small Evan-Thomas bowl (Plate 11/13 and 11/25) is shown for comparative purposes.

Plate 11/24. One tray and three coasters, all English. The tray, in mahogany with a dished top and a fine raised rim, has faded with time and light to develop a fine patina looking rather like walnut. c.1780. 18½in. in diameter. This was previously the top of a tripod wine table, evidence of that construction being apparent underneath. The dished shape of this piece was seemingly not echoed on platters of the period. On the tray is an unusually large mahogany coaster with a ⅜in. raised thin rim. The colour has faded on this more than on the flat surface. c.1840. 9in. in diameter. Next to it is a small finely turned bottle coaster, possibly in sycamore. c.1820. 3¾in. in diameter. At the back is a lignum vitae coaster with a finely turned everted rim which is concave beneath, making it very easy to pick up in use. c.1820. 10½in. in diameter.

Plate 11/25 (Opposite). A full frontal view of the small Evan-Thomas bowl previously described (Plate 11/13) to expose the surface patination in its full glory.

CHAPTER 12
Nutcrackers

Plate 12/1. English boxwood lever nutcracker, dated 1722 and initialled 'F.W.' 5¼in. x 2¼in.

Dated treen nutcrackers are known from the sixteenth century. These early ones were of levered type and designed to take small nuts such as hazel, also known as filberts because they ripened about St. Philbert's day. Nuts were collected from the wild and not cultivated so tended to be rather smaller than nuts commercially produced today. Walnuts were comparatively soft shelled and could be cracked in the teeth and were mostly too large to fit into the opening of the early nutcrackers. These elaborately carved lever nutcrackers often featured a human and occasionally an animal mask whose jaws opened by the lever mechanism to take the nut. In the early seventeenth century the lever nutcrackers sometimes had a bevelled recess between the levers sufficient to take a walnut and a little later screw action ones were made. Though metal nutcrackers were known in base metals from the fifteenth century, they only seem to have been extensively substituted for wooden ones in the seventeenth century.

The most elaborate and fine early nutcrackers were made in France of boxwood, though other continental countries, particularly Italy, also produced intricately

Plate 12/2. English lever yew wood nutcracker with the remarkably early date of 1708. The long-eared hare is rare, although squirrels are not uncommon. The particularly fine scratch-carved decoration on this example depicts a cat, bird, owl, snake, a shepherd with his crook and dog, as well as a fox with a bushy tail. 8in. x 3¼in.

Plate 12/2A. Detail of the nutcracker in Plate 12/2.

carved specimens. Due to their tight grain and resistence to fracturing, box and yew wood were the common timbers employed in the manufacture of nutcrackers. These same properties also facilitated the carver and contributed to the staggering longevity of these relatively simple devices.

The early English lever nutcrackers were characteristically decorated with the head of a man, often rather naïvely carved with a very flat face and little in the way of protruding features which would have been susceptible to damage. The overall shape tended to be rather square, contrasting with the Continental ones. The eyes were narrow, often lozenge or almond shaped, the ears rather flat and in low relief and the hair stylised. In contrast the French and Italian were more sophisticated, more

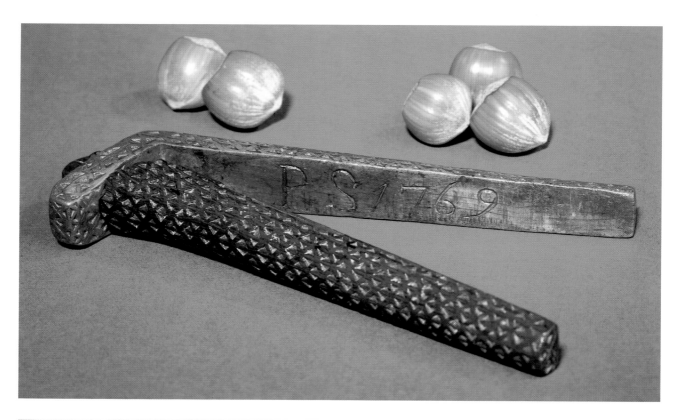

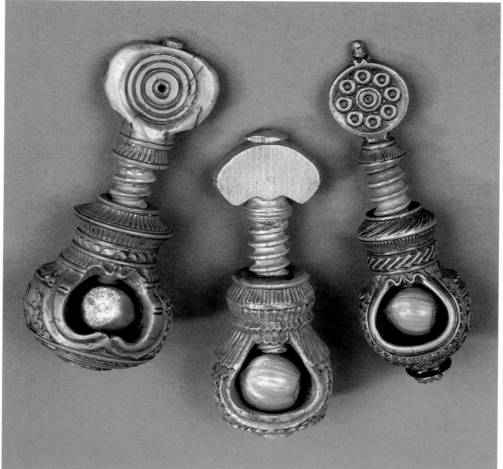

Plate 12/3. English chip-carved lever nutcracker, with contemporary date 1769, and initialled 'P.S'. One of a school of nut-crackers with overall chip-carved decoration dated between 1720 and 1770, making this a rather late example. One view is that this decoration might be a regional feature. 6in. x 1in.

Plate 12/4. Three specimen examples of screw-action nutcrackers, usually made of box. These are attributed variously to Switzerland, France and Germany. The aperture for the nut is often heart shaped and the decoration shows varying degrees of sophistication, usually with drilled roundels. The depth of carving, the shape of the aperture and the big roundel are all features of this Alpine style. It is unusual to find an example as large as the biggest shown here, which has a length of 4in. They usually date from the early to mid-19th century.

Plate 12/5. 1. English lever so-called 'pistol' nut cracker in boxwood with a rich colour. The style of the initials 'C.T.' suggests a date at least in the first quarter of the 18th century. 6in. x 1¾in. **2.** English yew wood lever nutcracker, initialled 'I + T'. Fine scratch carved decoration with trees, plants and flowers. The style of the script suggests a date in the first quarter of the 18th century. 6in. x 2½in.

elaborately, deeply and finely carved with the more protuberant nose and ears being liable to damage.

Another simple design was made using bent ash. This ingenious type exploits the natural flexibility of ash. An example is illustrated in Plate 12/17, 2.

Many screw action nutcrackers from the mid-seventeenth century and later survive. Many of them seem to have been made in a small size to fit into the pocket. It is extremely common to find teeth marks on the handles implying that the teeth were often used to get better leverage to crack the nut. As mentioned above, it must also be remembered that in the past nuts were considerably smaller. A collection of these small nutcrackers of many different designs is relatively easy to acquire in England though it is said to be much more difficult in the USA or Europe. They make a very good

display and are of considerable social interest. It is said that eating nuts was a popular pastime at theatrical performances based on the finding of large quantities of hazel shells under the boards of the auditorium when theatrical sites have been excavated.

As usual with treen, the literature on nutcrackers is sparse. The reference to one American book is given in the appendix as well as two museums which have particularly good nutcracker collections. There is a flourishing 'Nutcracker' Society in Germany (c/o Klaus Rosolleck, Koldeweystrasse 4. 38126 Braunschweig) which tries to collate the information gleaned from its members. There is also a Nutcracker Collectors Club in the U.S.A. (Susan Otto, 12204 Fox Run Drive, Chesterland, OH 44026). I am not aware of any Nutcracker nor sadly any Treen Society in this country.

Plate 12/6. Five acorn nutcrackers in various woods from 2⅛in. to 4⅕in. length. Characteristically the handles of most are pitted, due to the user employing his teeth to gain a firmer grip on the handle. The octagonal example in boxwood is particularly well patinated. These vary in date from the late 18th to the mid-19th century.

Plate 12/7. Five pocket screw action nutcrackers primarily in boxwood and ash. The first is a love token with a heart-shaped handle, and the second is in the shape of a barrel. These are said to have been designed to slip into the pocket, and it is suggested that, just as some people eat popcorn in cinemas today, in the eighteenth and nineteenth centuries it was popular to eat hazel nuts at theatrical performances. 1780-1850.

Plate 12/8. 1. Small English yew wood lever nutcracker with the particularly early date of 1669 and inscribed 'George Banister'. Details of the carving are shown, and include an old man, a monkey, a swan and other birds, a fox, a cock, a bearded patriarch as well as two heads of children(?) at the ends of the handles. There is also a wonderful heart pierced by arrows on the 'mallet' end. 4¼in. x 1½in.

Plates 12/8A to 12/8C (Left). Details of nutcracker illustrated in Plate 12/8.

Plate 12/9 (Right). Typical rather flat and broad, painted lever nutcracker with its hands to the side, thought to have been made in the Groden area of Germany from about 1780-1830. 10½in. x 4in.

Plate 12/10 (Below). Very finely carved French nutcracker in boxwood, probably made between 1570-1620. The significance of the bird on the head is uncertain but might be heraldic. It has a wonderfully rich colour and has survived undamaged. Note the prominent facial features associated with continental examples.

Plates 12/10A and 12/10B (Below, right). Details of the nutcracker illustrated in Plate 12/10. Note the handles incorporate whistling devices.

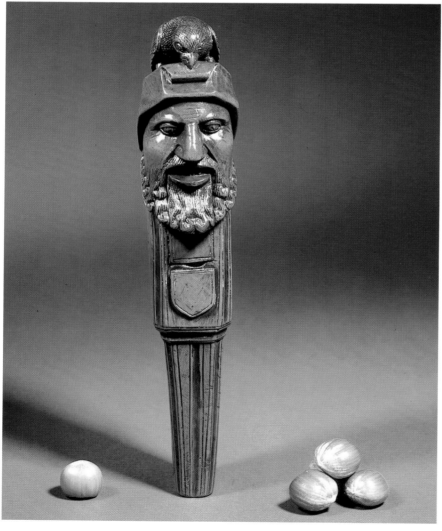

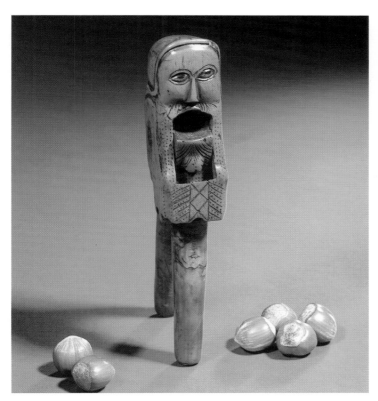

Plate 12/11. English boxwood lever nutcracker with typical rather flat face and simple line and dot decoration. This type, from the evidence of other dated examples, may have been made in the last quarter of the 17th century or the first quarter of the 18th. 7½in. x 1¼in.

Plate 12/12. Wonderful English boxwood lever nutcracker initialled 'RD' and 'RM' and dated 1688. This date appears to be contemporary with the second set of initials (RM), implying that it was initially carved earlier in the 17th century. Notice the rather flat face, square overall shape and stylised hair which are all characteristic of early English nutcrackers. 7in. x 2in.

Plates 12/12A and 12/12B. Details of the nutcracker illustrated in Plate 12/12.

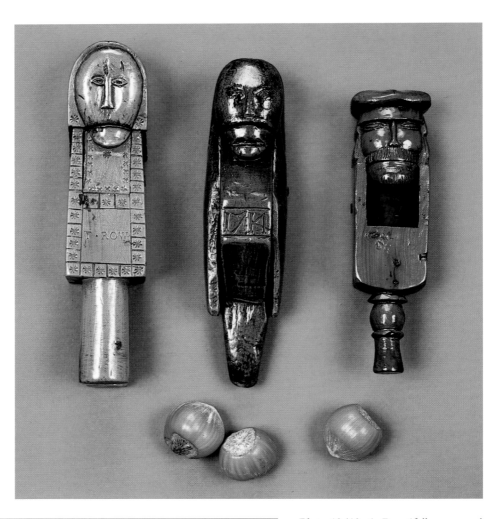

Plate 12/13. 1. Beautifully preserved English nutcracker in boxwood with unusual punched decoration and inscribed 'T.Row'. The flat face and very fine stylised hair with a rather square shape are again evident. This dates to the first half of the 18th century. 5in. x 1in. **2.** English walnut lever nutcracker dated 1714. Though rather damaged it still retains the characteristics features. 4½in. x 1¼in. **3.** Unusual yew wood nutcracker with the carved mask of a man with a flat hat and moustache. One lever is missing, the remaining one doubling as a pipe tamper. The carving is more detailed, deeper and sophisticated than the typical English ones of about 1700 raising the possibility that its origin might be the Low Countries. The layered hair is particularly unusual for an English example. 4in. x 1in.

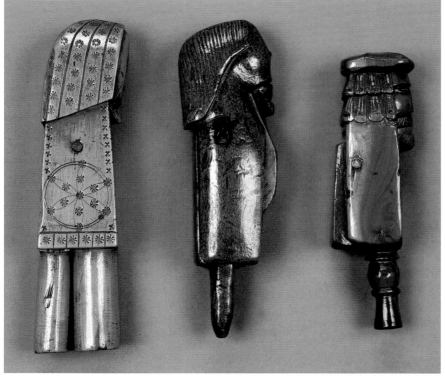

Plate 12/13A. Side views of the nutcrackers illustrated in Plate 12/13.

Plate 12/14. English yew wood lever nutcracker, sadly with one handle missing, with a wonderful flat face, cavalier moustache and inlaid holly eyes. Probably carved around 1700. 4¼in. x 1in.

Plate 12/15. Rather primitively carved English lever boxwood nut-cracker dated 1724, with great charm in spite of its missing handle. The fascinating speculation about this piece is whether the four faces represent a man, his wife and two children or whether they have some other significance. 6¼in. x 1¼in.

Plates 12/15A-D. Other views of the nutcracker in Plate 12/15.

Plate 12/16. 1. Small simple lever nutcracker initialled 'W.M.', with complex chip-carving and scratch-carved decoration including the figure of a woman in a crinoline. It is unusual to have both chip- and scratch-carving on the same piece. It probably dates c.1700 and is possibly sailor made. 4½in. x 1½in. **2.** Simple chip-carved love token nutcracker initialled 'EB. MB.' Lovely colour. First half of 18th century. 4½in. x ½in.

Plate 12/16A. Another view of the nut-crackers in Plate 12/16.

Plate 12/17. 1. Unusual English yew wood screw type nutcracker with slightly primitive lion finial. c.1800. 5in. x 1½in. **2.** Very good example of a simple ash nutcracker, late 18th/early 19th century, made from a single piece of wood. Ash is a wood known to bend well and retain its shape. Even so they tend to be rather delicate at the hinge so it is splendid to see one undamaged. 5in. long. **3.** Simple cross-over boxwood nutcracker with a carved finial and of lovely colour, probably from the first half of the 18th century. Ex-Shepherd Collection no. NUT 2012. 5½in. x 1¼in.

Plate 12/18. 1. English oak nutcracker with a bold ball finial on one handle. This is an Arts and Crafts Movement piece taking inspiration from early English ones shown elsewhere. This is a late derivative piece that lacks appeal. 6in. x 1½in. **2.** Rather crudely carved mid-19th century English sycamore nutcracker with original green paint that is characteristic of its type and was probably sold at fairgrounds. 5¼in. x 1½in.

Plate 12/19 (Above). A very fine example of a French screw type nutcracker with the maker's name 'Souan' inscribed on the handle. Made from burr box with marine ivory embellishments and in perfect condition. It is delightful to find signed pieces and further research may reveal the place and date that Souan worked. Probably made in the early 19th century. 5⅛in. x 1¾in.

Plate 12/20 (Below). Three nutcrackers of similar though simpler style than the finest shown in the previous plate and again here (left). The second nutcracker, also inscribed 'Souan' on the handle, is of burr box but with horn embellishments. The third is altogether simpler but still has the typical ovoid decorated opening. The last and simplest doesn't have this feature and may be from a different workshop. 19th century.

Plate 12/21. Fine quality lever nutcracker with a wonderful colour. The naturalistic hair, the style and decoration of the handle incorporating stylised acanthus leaves is a classical baroque form characteristic of a French or Italian origin and date it to the mid-17th century. It also has an interesting old metal repair. 5¾in. x 1½in.

Plate 12/21A. Another view of Plate 12/21.

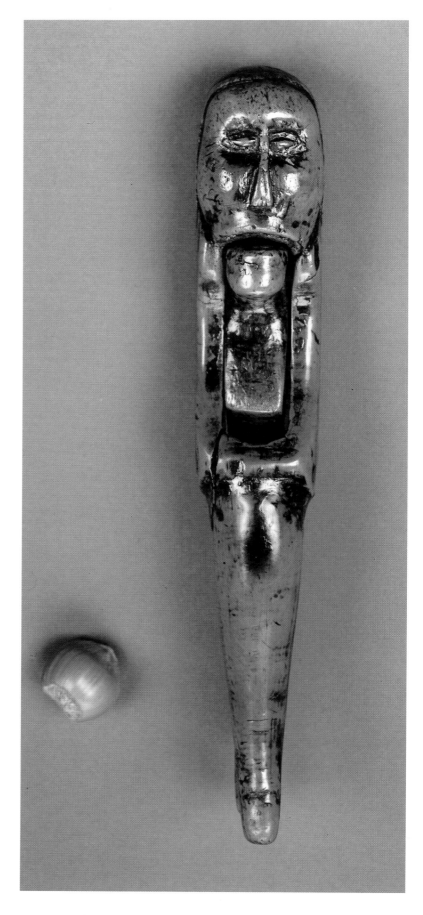

Plate 12/22. Unusual English, lignum vitae, engine turned, screw type acorn nutcracker. c.1700. 2½in. x 1¼in.

Plate 12/23. English boxwood nutcracker of particularly fine colour with the figure of a gaunt and very worried looking man. c.1670. 7¾in. x 1¾in.

Plate 12/24. English boxwood nutcracker with chip-carved and incised decoration of serpents and with the particularly early date of 1612 and initialled 'RS'. 7½in. long.

Plate 12/24A. Detail of the nutcracker in Plate 12/24.

Plate 12/25. 1. English screw type nutcracker, possibly in faded walnut, of rather larger size than most illustrated here indicating it was not just for cracking hazel nuts. However, the opening is still rather small for the best walnuts now available in your supermarket. Late 18th century. 5½in. x 1½in. **2.** English nutcracker in walnut with scalloped and beaded decoration as well as the usual teeth marks on the handle. First quarter 18th century. 3¼in. x 1½in.

CHAPTER 13

Lemon Squeezers

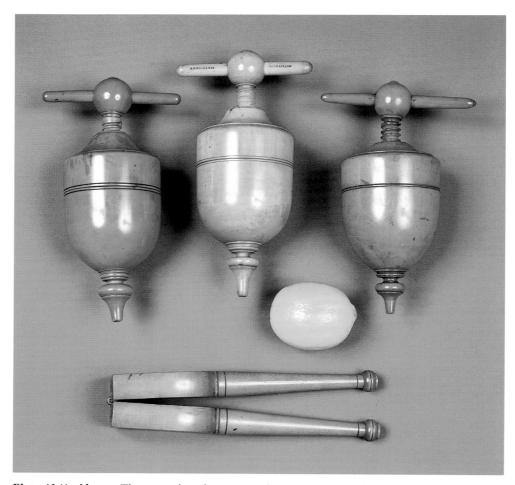

Plate 13/1. Above. Three urn-shaped screw type lemon squeezers in boxwood. The centre one is engraved B.B. Wells, 431, West Strand. They are shown together to illustrate the theory that they were made in the same workshop. 19th century. 7½in. long. **Below.** A robust boxwood lever action lemon squeezer which is rather small for the current breed of lemon shown. 19th century. 8½in. long.

Lemons are known to have been imported into England at least from the seventeenth century. Three types of squeezers are known, lever, screw and scoop. The lever ones are not particularly elegant, usually being more functional than decorative. The screw ones above appear to have been mainly nineteenth century or later and three have been included to show their typical form. The scoop type in contrast comes in a variety of woods though most commonly box, and has delightful variation in patination, colour and age. Examples shown range from the eighteenth to twentieth centuries and are of a design that is still obtainable today. Part of their further attraction is that they are small objects that can easily be shown in a pleasing display without a vast financial outlay, yet are still evocative of a previous age. They can be found not only in antique shops, but centres, fairs, markets and car boot sales, which

Plate 13/2. Seventeen scoop type lemon squeezers in box, fruitwood and sycamore. The central one is most beautifully turned and may well be 18th century. The remainder are 19th century, though showing variable signs of age and use. Around 5in. to 5½in. long.

gives the collector the very important added value and fun of the thrill of the chase. Though many of these must have been made in large numbers by particular craft workshops there remain many variations in the details of style.

In contrast Plate 13/1 shows three urn-shaped, screw type squeezers which, though having minor differences, must have been made in the same workshop. The top unscrews or has a ratchet type connector. The handle is attached to a long screw with a knob on the end to crush the lemon and allow the juice to run from the spout at the bottom. This style was always made of boxwood. Interestingly, one of them is named: B.B. Wells, 431, West Strand. Investigation has not yet revealed whether he was the maker or the retailer. The duration of this firm's existence is unknown.

Plate 14/1. Top row. 1. English fruitwood egg cup with carved decoration to the bowl. and a slightly domed foot. First quarter 19th century. 2⅜in. x 1¾in. **2.** English egg cup with domed foot and knop. 19th century. 3½in. x 2in. **3.** Very early English pole lathe turned walnut egg cup with particularly attractive wear, colour and appearance. It has a well worn knop and an early domed foot which would support a date of the last quarter 17th century. 3⅞in. x 2in. **4.** English pole lathe turned fruitwood egg cup from the mid-19th century. 3¾in. x 1⅞in. **5.** English walnut egg cup with steeply domed foot reminiscent of renaissance turning but probably early 19th century. 4½6in. x 2in. **6.** English lignum egg cup. 19th century. 3in. x 1½in.

Bottom row. 1 and 5. A pair of English mahogany urn-shaped egg cups, mid-19th century. 3in. x 2in. **2 and 4.** A pair of yew wood egg cups of unusual form. Mid-19th century. 4in. x 2¼in. **3.** English fruitwood egg cup (probably plum) with unusually large base. 19th century. 2½in. x 3¼in.

Plate 14/2 (Left). Thirteen pairs of egg cups, all 19th century.

Plate 14/3 (Opposite). Thirty 19th century egg cups. The top row are mainly urn shaped. The fourth is oak with a stepped and domed foot, a slim knop and is probably the earliest. The second row shows many variations in the colour of simple sycamore egg cups and the third row shows some of the variety of woods, shapes and sizes. The bottom row shows further variety in the egg cups, two having particularly large bases; particularly the seventh which, unusually, is in lignum vitae.

CHAPTER 14

Egg Cups

Sixty-seven egg cups, many in pairs, are illustrated here, to show something of their variety. They can be found in specially designed stands which are usually Victorian though occasionally delightful Georgian examples come to light. Many different woods were used and there is a large range of styles and sophistication. These survivors predominantly have the appearance of being nineteenth century but are notoriously difficult to date more accurately. The illustrations also show what an attractive display can be made from a collection of such simple objects.

CHAPTER 15

Miscellaneous

Wine Tasters, Apple Corers, Dish Slopes, Funnels, Negus Strainers,
a Jug and various other objects

In this chapter a wide variety of objects have been included that are in some way related to food or drink that don't fit easily under the previous chapter headings. They illustrate the enormous range of objects beyond the obvious eating and drinking vessels produced by the turner from his wood.

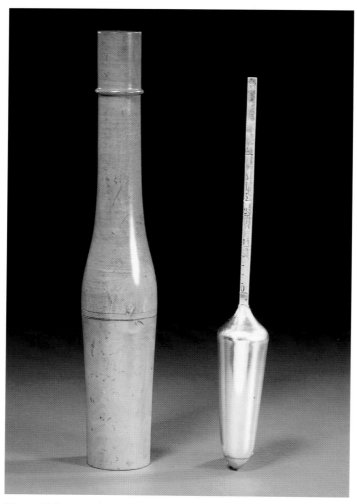

Plate 15/1. French silver milk densitometer in boxwood case. Used for testing the specific gravity of milk to see whether it had been adulterated with water. 8¾in. x 1¼in.

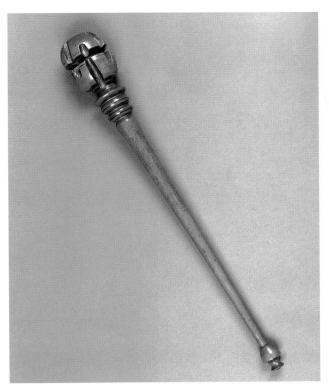

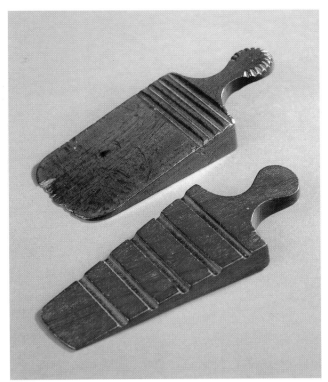

Plate 15/2 (Above). English fruitwood chocolate whisk of lovely weight and colour dating from around 1770-80.

Plate 15/3 (Above right). Two 19th century mahogany dish slopes. These were used to tilt the plate to scoop out the juices. **Above.** Very good Cuban mahogany dish slope with appealing chip-carved decoration and concave under surface to handle (not seen in illustration). 6½in. long. **Below.** A Honduran mahogany dish slope with no patination, a plain design with no attractive redeeming features. These two slopes illustrate to a budding collector what to get and what to leave. 6½in. long.

Plate 15/4. Three English dish slopes to illustrate some of the different styles and sizes made. All 19th century, though **1** appears to be the earliest. Note the rich colour and different design of the handles of the first two compared to the first in the previous plate. **1.** Mahogany initialled FB on base. ¾in. x 7in. **2.** Mahogany with rather interesting shallow stepped design. ¾in. x 7in. **3.** Small example in stained oak. ½in. x 4in.

Plate 15/5. 1. Possibly a unique Welsh jug with original paint and satisfying artistry in the production of the beautiful curves of its body and handle. This is a classic pottery shape following the fashion of the period (mid–19th century). We have seen no comparable examples. 8¼in. x 2in.

Plate 15/6. Graduated dumbbell shaped glass balls with 'toggle' in turned box. These were used to measure the specific gravity of spirits and hence its alcohol content. The illustration shows three balls at slightly different levels in three star Martell brandy. 19th century. (For a comparable set see Pinto page 278.)

Plate 15/7. Funnels. **1.** 19th century sycamore funnel, with no patination. 6½in. x 3¾in. **2.** Top half only of wonderfully patinated, finely turned sycamore funnel. 2½in. x 4in. **3.** 19th century sycamore funnel, with good colour and therefore substantially more desirable than the first example. 6in. x 3½in. **4.** 19th century beech funnel made from a single piece of wood. 5¼in. x 3¾in. **5.** Very tactile elm funnel, probably 19th century. 4½in. x 2¾in. **6.** Sycamore strainer funnel with original mesh. 5¾in. x 2¾in. **7.** Horrid funnel, stained by ignorant individual to an unappealing brown, presumably with intent to pretend it has some age. Only included because its shape is different and to demonstrate that not all wooden objects are attractive.

Plate 15/8. Three wine tasters. **1.** A much used English sycamore wine taster showing all the right features of wear in the expected places. Mid-18th century. 1¼in. x 4in. (including handle). **2.** 18th century twin-handled shallow bowl possibly for wine or spirit tasting. This interesting object bears remarkable similarity to the form of negus strainers. Possibly walnut. 1in. x 8½in. **3.** Wine taster covered in carved decoration with the remnants of old gesso covering the inside of the bowl. The attraction of this piece is enhanced by the wear and carving in particular. Early 18th century. 1in. x 3⅜in. (including handle).

Plate 15/8A. Carved decoration on the underside of the third wine taster.

Plate 15/9. An unusual English burr maple wood wine taster of generous proportions. The well-shaped handle has a large hole through which, tradition dictates, the 'sommelier' would tie a cord and attach it to his belt. Mid-17th century. 1¾in. x 3½in. at the rim.

Plate 15/10. Three negus strainers. **1.** English negus strainer in finely figured fruitwood with a turned pierced bowl and shaped moulded handles. This is almost identical to the one sold in the Shepherd Collection sale at Sotheby's, lot 218, which at that time had the Evan-Thomas Collection label no. 642 (plate 61 in his book). However, the size of that was said to be 8in. while this is just under 8in. The holes are probably in the same places. This may be the Evan-Thomas piece but is possibly another made at about the same time by the same turner. Early 18th century. 8in. x 3¾in. **2.** English turned fruitwood negus strainer with thin shaped handles. Early 18th century. 7in. x 3½in. **3.** Rare English sycamore negus strainer turned from a huge block of wood without any damage to its handles despite its age and fineness. It has probably survived in this pristine condition because it had only minimal use or was repeatedly washed, thus accounting for the lack of patination. c.1780. 14½in. long.

Plate 15/10A. Detailed picture to show the way these strainers may have been made. The top and bottom ones show apparent turning lines between the two flanges which contrasts with the centre one which has clear surface marking indicating where the flange was cut away. These observations are difficult to explain as it has always been assumed that these thin handled objects were turned with a complete circular flange or collar, most of which was then cut away to form the handles. It would have been a remarkable turner, even on a pole lathe, to turn in the area between the handles. Further study of this point on a larger number of strainers is required before any firm conclusions can be reached.

Plate 15/11. Three apple corers or cheese samplers with an English apple to give an indication of their size. These corers may have been used for either purpose depending on their size. The largest, because of its size, must have been made as a cheese scoop and is in walnut. Though of rather similar design to the next one it has not been so finely turned and is less elegant an object. Probably last quarter 18th century. 8in. long. The central one has been well used, is made from a fruit wood and has graduated turned bands with incised decoration to the handle terminating in a bold knop. The fine turning and design make this an elegant piece. Mid-18th century. 6¼in. long. The third (nearest the camera) is chip-carved in fruitwood dated 1706 and engraved Anne, surmounted with what might be a ladle. It shows few signs of wear and may have been a love token from a Welsh chap hoping for some good cooking.

Plate 15/12. A small chip-carved apple corer c.1780. 3½in. x ½in.

Plate 15/13. English mahogany 19th century rotating coaster, probably for cheese, with some late 20th century Shropshire blue. The coaster is built to rotate on its spindle. 1¼in. x 8¾in.

Plate 15/14. Wine bottle corker in sycamore. The metal–lined tunnel through the centre is slightly tapered to compress the cork during its insertion. Late 19th century.

Plate 15/15. A large late 17th century spirit or pilgrim flask of massive proportions with turned and chip-carved decoration. Previously in the Pitt Rivers Collection and documented as Scottish. c.1680. 13½in. x 3in.

Plate 15/16. A rare survival of a European pilgrim's flask, in sycamore or plane tree, with holes in the neck for a leather carrying strap. c.1800. (See Pinto plate 53e for a similar example.) 13½in. x 3½in.

Plate 15/17. Two footed dishes that could have been used for sweetmeats. The lighter one, with a strikingly everted rim, is probably made from pearwood and dates from around 1870. The patination on the foot is particularly pleasing. 3¾in. x 4½in. at the rim. The darker one has a wide shallow bowl on a pedestal stem and a rich deep conker colour. It is probably made from fruitwood and dates from c.1750.

Plate 15/18. An English fruit-wood bowl and cover with an oriental shape dating from c.1780. A lovely finely turned object but its function must have been more than decorative. Maybe it was an early treen sugar bowl. 4½in. x 5in. at the rim.

CHAPTER 16

What on Earth was it used for?

Treen objects were made for a specific purpose. With most of the objects illustrated in this book, that function is obvious, though the detail may be uncertain – for example, whether a particular mortar and pestle was for snuff or apothecary's use. However, one comes across things that are attractive in some way, are beautifully turned, show interesting wear, have ancient repairs, have lustrous patination, are tactile, but their use is not apparent and they are therefore a challenge. Some collectors may not be interested in the object's function, only in its aesthetic appeal. Objects are shown in this chapter that may have some or all of these other attributes but universally have no obvious specific function. If you have firm ideas on their purpose, function or other information about them, please write.

Plate 16/1. A remarkable elaborately and finely turned ash cup, possibly Welsh, c.1700. It demonstrates fine turning marks on the base. The cup is 1in. deep, with encrustations (from salt?) on the bottom coinciding with the changing colour seen on its bowl. Could this have been a rather elaborately carved salt? If not, what was its purpose? This is a tactile piece, well patinated and with a glorious colour. 6½in. x 2¼in.

Plate 16/2. English oak cup and cover, whose style suggests that it is a copy of a c.1600 communion wafer cup, with its classical shape. The turning is excellent, and the date is perhaps 1800. This is probably a communion cup, but could it be a covered salt? 9½in. x 3¼in.

Plate 16/3. 1. English lignum vitae bowl with a crenellated rim on a stem with ring-turned decoration to the bowl and foot. Could it have been for sugar or sweetmeats? Early 19th century. 4¾in. x 4¾in. **2.** Lignum vitae bowl on a foot with no stem and a very rich variegated colour. It is too deep to be a salt, the ribbed lip was not designed for drinking and it never had a lid. So what is it? There is a circumferential shadow 1in. below the rim on the inside of the bowl suggesting it may have been used with liquids, though not necessarily as its original purpose. Could it have been for sugar or sweetmeats? 5½in. x 2in.

Plate 16/4. 1. A richly coloured English cedar cup that may have lost its cover, 4in. high with a well defined disc knopped stem that suggests a date around 1780. Could it have been a spice pot? Did it originally have a glass or silver liner for mustard or another condiment? **2.** A rather sallow yew wood container with a deep tapering bowl not fully shown in this picture, 2½in. high, but its nationality and function are not obvious. A glass holder has been suggested but this doesn't seem very convincing. **3.** An elegantly pole lathe turned fruitwood 'holder', possibly for salt, or was it really a stand for a glass bowl for magnifying light as used by lace makers? And is it English or French? **4.** A mahogany pot, 2½in. high, of about 1850 with original pale polished gesso which some vandal has attempted to remove. This is probably too deep to be a salt and may be medical or scientific, but for what?

Plate 16/5 (Left). A tall pearwood cup and cover with a domed lid surmounted with a finial. It has a typical neo-classical urn shape. The rich patination is lighter in colour on the short stem, round the body and on the finial. c.1790. This seems to be rather large (height 8½in.) to be a jar for expensive spices though this may have been its purpose. The rim under the cover (not shown) precludes its use as a drinking vessel. The final thought is whether it could have been a tea caddy or an early sugar urn. These gradually superseded casters towards the end of the 18th century, and there are silver precedents of this style from the late 18th century.

Plate 16/6 (Above). Small polychromed pole lathe turned pot with screw-on lid, c.1720, bought described as an English spice pot, but could it be Indian and what was it used for? 1¾in. x 2⅝in.

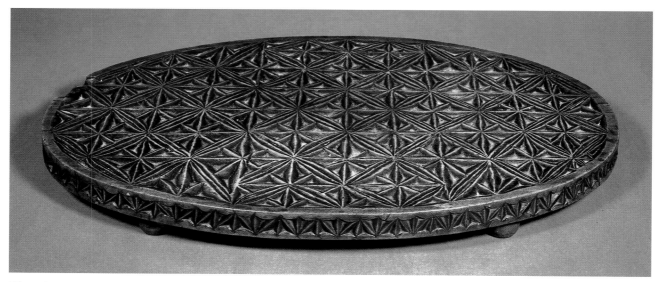

Plate 16/7. Large, extensively chip-carved 'mat' on four ball feet. Is it a rimless coaster, or a serving stand for putting hot pans on, or what? Please help. Is it Welsh or Friesland and sailor made? Oval, 18in. x 12in. c.1820/30.

Plate 16/8. Ornately and meticulously turned object which comes apart as shown. This has clearly been designed for a specific purpose, the nature of which remains a mystery. The small hole shown on the front of the base must have had some function, so too the eccentric pin in the top cavity. Its style suggests a date of 1780. Nobody who has seen it has any idea as to its original purpose. What do you think it was made for? 5in. x 2⅛in.

CHAPTER 17

Old Repairs

Plate 17/1. Detail from Roundel case shown in Plate 10/1 to show in close-up the ancient stapled repair with the discoloration of the surrounding wood caused by leaching of iron from the staple. It happens to show the burned incised decoration rather well.

A bad split or damage to a treen object considerably lessens its attraction and value. However, to expect pieces of everyday treen to have survived tens if not hundreds of years in totally pristine condition is unrealistic. There is a thin dividing line between acceptable wear and damage in the normal course of an object's life and damage that is sufficiently severe to detract from its appeal. Old splits or damage that has been repaired in the distant past may considerably enhance its character and not be detrimental to its value. A bad split repaired in an interesting way years ago may be very much more desirable than an unrepaired one.

Thus this chapter illustrates some of the interesting old repairs that have been encountered.

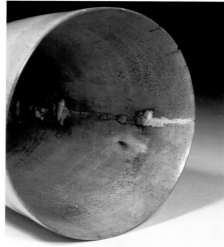

Plate 17/2. Details of the old stitched repair to the lámhóg shown in Plate 4/4. This very old repair was clearly successful in making the vessel 'beer tight' again and has been done with thin slivers of willow. It also indicates the value that was attached to such objects as, despite extensive splitting down one side and into the base, it was thought worthy of repair and continued use.

188

Plate 17/3. Staples have been used for this old repair to the Irish lámhóg previously shown in Plate 4/3. Somehow they are sympathetic to the general feeling of age in this vessel.

Plate 17/4. Detail of old wired repair of cup shown in Plate 3/11 showing discoloration of the wood from long-standing leaching out of the iron as well as details of the incised decoration.

Plate 17/5. Old twisted wire repair to the early pearwood cup shown in Plate 3/21.

Plate 17/6. Silver wire repair to thin split in this early 'monks' mazer bowl illustrated in Plate 3/1.

Plate 7/7. Intriguing old string and wire repairs to an old and battered scoop or ladle shown in Plate 9/18. Despite the relative simplicity of the object it was sufficiently treasured and valued to be repaired even in this rather wizened state. Though this piece has the scars of a long and hard life it deserves cherishing in its decline.

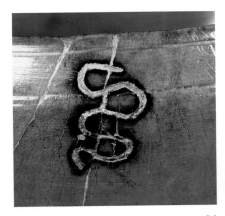

Plate 7/8. A tortuous and very successful old repair to a split bowl (Plate 11/21) using iron wire. Over the years the iron has leached out discolouring the surrounding wood, even permeating the full thickness of the wall to leave a wormlike impression on the inside.

Plate 7/9. A close-up picture of the twisted wire repair to the Norwegian drinking bowl illustrated in Plate 3/52. This, incidentally, shows the patination and one of the dates – 1761.

CHAPTER 18

Cautionary Tales

Plate 18/1. A recently turned wild cherry bowl showing the shrinkage across the grain within a few weeks in an object that has been turned 'in the green' with unseasoned wood. Measurements are 4⅜in. x 5½₆in. at the rim and 2¼in. x 2⅛in. at the base.

British or Foreign?

There is a considerable quantity of both turned and carved wooden ware on the market at the present time, Afghan particularly, but also African, Indian and Continental. This may be partly because much of it is very attractive craft work from other cultures but also because of the increasing difficulty in finding English treen to collect or sell. Some of the Afghan material, in particular, shows signs of considerable age, has been attractively pole lathe turned, often with evidence of shrinkage across the grain, has acquired a rich patination and overall is often very attractive. Its large scale importation is a very recent phenomenon.

Many collectors and dealers are not familiar with the range of objects from abroad and it has taken time for everyone to develop the appropriate knowledge. It may be a perfectly honest matter of opinion whether a small wooden object without provenance or other known examples is British or imported. The simple tools of everyday life were commonly made of wood in most cultures and the design and form can be similar. Look, for instance, at Plate 9/18 (left), showing a ladle that would pass a hundred eyes (both dealers and collectors!) as British, probably Welsh, yet was bought in a market in Italy making it likely, but not certain, that it is Italian.

Whilst there is no reason against buying European or any other nationality treen it is important to note the price differentials.

Shrinkage Across the Grain – A Reliable Guide to Age?

There is a very widespread belief that with the passage of time an object turned in the round gradually becomes oval. Many collectors and dealers look to this shrinkage as a reliable sign of age, often basing their judgement of an item's antiquity on its deviation from its original circular shape. This can be misleading. When wood is seasoned it naturally shrinks across the grain as it dries. The main determinant, therefore, of an object's deviation from the circular is the time and effectiveness of seasoning prior to

Plate 18/2. A lidded bowl and jug. The bowl is pole lathe turned, with very attractive marking and patination, and stands 6in. high. It was sold some years ago as an English dry storage jar c.1800. The wood has a typical Afghan appearance though the chuck marks could be British. A considerable time later an almost identical one was found – not in such pristine condition but this time heavily perfumed with Indian spices leading to the conclusion that they were probably both Afghan.

The little jug, extensively chip carved over the body, was carved and not turned. The form is derived from known English pottery shapes from the mid-19th century. The wood is of uniform colour and not particularly close grained. It is probably African, made for the European market. So, though it is of British form, it is of less interest to a collector of treen predominantly from the British Isles.

turning. If an object is turned from very well seasoned wood there may be little change in its shape even after two hundred years. However, many objects, particularly everyday ones, were turned 'in the green', that is essentially without any seasoning or drying. 'Green' wood is often much easier to turn and the shrinkage that occurs over days or weeks *(not years)* as it dries out often leads to considerable shrinkage and sometimes deformity. Plate 18/1 illustrates this point. When this cherrywood bowl was turned in the green by a living turner in about 1994 it was circular. Within a few weeks it had become oval as shown. Its measurements now (1997) are 4⅜in. x 5⅟₁₆in. across the rim and 2⅛in. and 2½in. across the base, quantitating what the photograph reveals.

Thus the most important factor determining shrinkage after turning is how well seasoned, and thus how dry, it was at the moment of creation. However, this is not the only factor. Different woods will shrink in the seasoning process considerably more than others and there is no reason why further drying and therefore shrinkage can't take place after turning. Just remember not to over-emphasise the importance of shrinkage as a reliable indicator of age.

Fakes and Deception

As in many areas of art and antiques, faking and deception may become prevalent if that type of object becomes desirable and expensive. Overt faking has probably been quite uncommon with treen as the effort and skill required didn't make the project worthwhile.

There are exceptions, however, perhaps the most frequently quoted being square platters with turned salt concavities. These are simple to make, command high prices because of their rarity if genuine and have been extensively faked. Experience and judgement play a crucial role in assessing whether the wear is appropriate for a 17th century or earlier piece. On the other hand it is unlikely that a James I armorial standing cup has been faked because of the enormous amount of highly skilled intricate work that would be required.

To the collector appropriate signs of wear, age and a long and useful life can be the very features that make an object desirable. To distinguish these from deliberate distressing may sometimes be easy but is often very difficult, even to the experienced professional. Thus the faker and over-enthusiastic restorer pit their skills against the punter trying to build up a collection of genuinely old treen.

A few examples of cautionary tales are illustrated.

Plate 18/3 (Above). Two pole lathe turned bowls with deeply incised decoration to the interior, particularly obvious on the larger bowl. This also has incredible wear, as can be seen in the inside where the turning marks have been obliterated in a patchy manner, presumably from use, leaving a very gnarled surface of considerable interest. The appearance of the wood, particularly on the base, confirms the suspicion that these are likely to be obscure hardwood from Afghanistan.

Plate 18/4 (Left). Two platters shown to illustrate the difference between the very varied length, direction and depth of knife marks readily accepted as normal usage (left) contrasted with the regular uniform 'scoring' marks on the other. Their regularity, evenness of depth and direction raise one's suspicions these were distressed to simulate age.

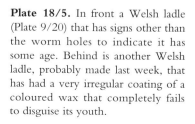

Plate 18/5. In front a Welsh ladle (Plate 9/20) that has signs other than the worm holes to indicate it has some age. Behind is another Welsh ladle, probably made last week, that has had a very irregular coating of a coloured wax that completely fails to disguise its youth.

CHAPTER 19

Surfaces

The surface appearance of a piece of treen is dependent on many factors including the underlying wood, its original and later treatments with varnish, paint and/or wax polish. It may have been in contact with water or other liquids. The wear and tear it has received over the years, as well as the care or neglect that it has survived, all have a major impact on the present surface appearance.

The majority of treen objects were originally varnished. Over the years this may have altered in different ways. Lignum vitae, which retains its characteristic odour for hundreds of years, is a particularly oily wood. This may be the basis for the poor sticking properties of varnish and frequently one sees areas of slight yellowness which, though raising the suspicion that the piece could previously have been gilded, are usually due to degradation of the varnish. However, as commented on by Pinto, water may seep into cracks in the varnish and in its subsequent degradation it reveals an almost golden colour which is slightly accentuated by the warm colour of the photographs used to illustrate the point. The microscope is particularly helpful, without doing any detailed chemical analysis, in trying to sort out the basis of the current surface appearance.

Careful examination with a hand lens of many pieces made from lignum vitae will reveal areas of degraded

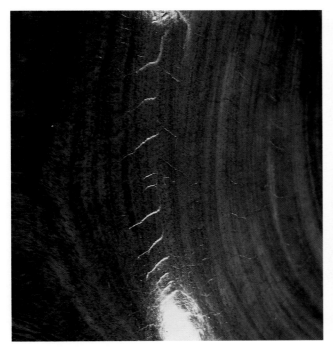

Plate 19/1. Close-up photograph of the wassail bowl shown bottom left in Plate 1/2 to demonstrate the superficial 'craquelure' appearance one loves to find as it may be an indicator of considerable age, in this case mid-17th century.

Plate 19/2. This is a detailed picture of the oak salt shown in Plate 7/3 to show the appearance of the grain. This is characteristic of old oak which has been soaked in water and later waxed and cherished as the history of this piece records. It goes grey from the wetness but then develops this milky colour with reversal of the expected colour of the open grain. As the photograph shows, the open grain instead of being lighter is in fact now darker in colour.

Plate 19/3. This shows a close-up of the inside of the salt shown in Plate 7/7 to emphasise the ageing, turning and years of accumulated "gunk". This is a highly desirable piece of treen to connoisseurs of ageing. Keep it well away from anyone suggesting it should be stripped.

Plate 19/4. A close-up of the platter seen in Plate 11/7 showing surface detail and patination that has accumulated from years of use.

Plate 19/5. The knop on the lid of the wassail bowl shown in Plate 1/2. This shows clear evidence of gold leaf when examined under the microscope. Whether this was originally gilded or a later addition cannot be determined. No evidence of gold leaf has been found elsewhere on the bowl, the other areas of 'yellowness' being attributable to degraded varnish.

varnish. So frequent is this finding that its absence suggests either that the piece is relatively youthful or that it has been stripped.

In truth, the ageing of the varnish is one of the most important elements that make up patina. Good patination is almost a prerequisite for desirability and thus collectability and has been one of the main criteria in selecting objects to buy for my own collection. This is particularly well shown in Plate 19/16 where the extremes of a very flat uninteresting surface on a perfectly good sycamore platter contrasts with the incredible wear, irregularity and colour of another sycamore platter of similar form. They could even be of similar age.

Many old pieces of lignum vitae also show a superficial craquelure which is illustrated in Plate 19/1. Other than age, the determinants of this appearance are uncertain. I have found it to be universal in seventeenth century lignum vitae objects but no detailed study has been done with dated pieces to establish the truth of the suggestion that this could be predominantly age related.

Illustrated here are a variety of surfaces, not only the exquisite, mind-bogglingly wonderful ones but the uninteresting, mundane and flat to give you, the reader, the opportunity to assess our view.

Plate 19/6. Degraded varnish giving the golden colour to the stem of this lignum vitae possible sugar bowl shown in Plate 16/3. This appearance is common on a variety of lignum objects raising the speculation whether it is due to the particular varnish used or whether it has something to do with the oiliness or some other property of this particular wood. It is not due primarily to a build-up of wax, an opinion I have frequently heard reiterated.

Plate 19/7 (Above and left). Two views of the more extensively affected lignum vitae coffee grinder shown in Plate 8/18. Here it is much easier to see the thick layers of degraded varnish almost peeling off. Microscopic examination reveals very fine turning marks on the underlying timber with a layer of transparent varnish covered by another layer of yellowish varnish partly degraded and partly almost detached. Pinto tells us he would strip such a piece! No man is completely perfect but this is not advice we could support now – to put it at its mildest!

Plate 19/8. A wonderful patchy golden colour on the inside of the lignum vitae goblet shown in Plate 3/18, left. Under the microscope this can be seen to be made up of a combination of the underlying sapwood visible with and without varnish, the detached crazed varnish and the craquelure lower down. These features considerably add to its attraction.

Plate 19/9. The bottom of the inside of the large posset bowl shown in Plate 1/17 where there is an irregular pock-marked area. Under the microscope this has the appearance of a pigment, presumably painted, with variably degraded varnish above and below. This is very striking as it is made from the plane tree and not lignum.

Plate 19/10. The edge of the foot of the same bowl to show the way the old varnish has crinkled with an alluring craquelure.

Plate 19/11. The lid of the tankard shown in Plate 3/5 which under the microscope shows varnish on top of a pigmented layer. The varnish does show considerable patchy degradation. There is however no pigmented layer over the basket work turning on the bowl.

Plate 19/12. The leading edge of the scoop shown in Plate 9/18, left. Under the microscope multiple layers can be seen, the underlying wood, paint and pigmented varnish.

Plate 19/13 (Above right). A closer view of the decoration on the James I standing cup of 1628 shown in Plate 3/20. This is meticulously done pyrography (writing in fire) or pokerwork. This craft was a widespread method of wood decoration throughout Europe and was popular in the early 17th century. It appears that the bolder lines may have been incised first and then burnt but in such a careful way that the incised edges have not been blurred. Examination of two cups of similar style in the British Museum shows that some of their decoration is incised but has not been burnt. This suggests that fine gouging was the initial form of decoration with subsequent pyrography which in some cups was not complete. The finer lines, such as on the leaves, have minimal depth suggesting they were only burnt. One can only marvel at the skill of this, done at a time when the instrument had to be heated repeatedly over charcoal. For a more detailed account of pyrography and how sophisticated it can be see *Tunbridge and Scottish Souvenir Woodware* by E.H. and Eva R. Pinto.

Plate 19/14. A close-up of the quaich shown in Plate 5/2 (6) which shows the texture and variations in colour of this sycamore object. No firm conclusions could be reached after microscopic examination as to whether there was paint or pigment in the varnish or whether the appearance was just due to its unusual whitish degradation. It is clearly an acquired surface possibly related to its years of use and washing.

Plate 19/15. The almost sandpaper-like finish or very fine craquelure on the surface of this early maple goblet shown on the right in Plate 3/18. This varnish was probably applied after cleaning because it is over the build-up of muck in the incised decoration. Though old this surface is not the original one.

Plate 19/16. Close-up of two platters both sycamore and of similar form to show the contrast between the left-hand one that must have led a rough but very interesting life (the deeply pitted wood and old varnish has led to this appearance) and the other which must have belonged to a very house proud woman who kept all her dishes in a state of perfect cleanliness – or rarely used them.

Plate 19/17. It is extremely rare to find this quality and condition of painted decoration on treen. Though it is often suggested that treen had been decorated frequently in this way few such examples survive. The painting is typical of English japanning dating from the first half of the 18th century. See Plate 3/25.

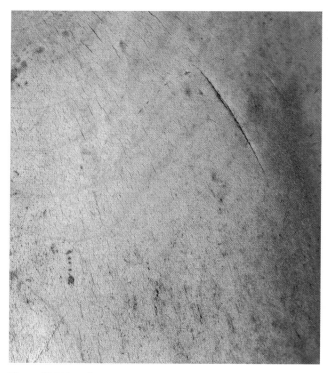

Plate 19/18. This semi-transparent filmy white appearance on the bowl in Plate 11/20 is often attributed to its repeated use with milk which is said to allow incorporation of casein into the surface of the sycamore so the grain is still visible beneath. The colour is rarely seen in anything other than objects that have been used in the dairy.

Plate 19/19. The pearwood goblet on the left has been recently stripped, the underlying surface now being completely raw. It will require years of polishing and exposure to acquire any skin. The fruitwood vessel on the right has a rich variegated colour, lacking on the goblet, making it considerably more interesting.

Plate 19/20. Three muffineers, all in sycamore. The one on the left has been given a uniform brown stain completely hiding its charm. The central one exudes character and charm and would be the obvious winner in any beauty contest. The one on the right has a relatively flat and uninteresting face and foot compared to her neighbours and wouldn't be chosen to be the receptionist in a Mayfair Beauty Salon.

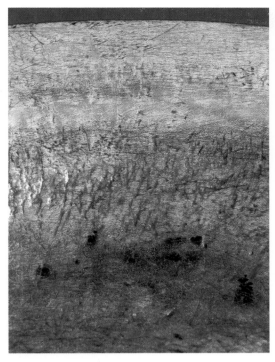

Plate 19/21. A close-up of the shallow dish shown in Plate 11/1. This really epitomises the best of patination and desirability with varying depths of wear and irregular luscious creamy speckled brownness.

Plate 19/22. A close-up view of three platters. The sycamore one on the left has a thick lustrous surface patination. That on the right has considerably less surface interest though some clear evidence of wear and age. The contrast between these two has been slightly reduced by the camera. The paler one behind is new, having recently been made from a lime tree at Hampton Court Palace blown down in the great gale of 1987 and has yet to acquire any signs of age or wear.

Plate 19/23. Contrast the rich patina of the goblet on the left (Plate 3/18) with the exceptionally flat surface of the salt on the right (Plate 7/18), both pieces being in lignum vitae.

Owen Evan-Thomas' Press Cutting Book

20 DOVER STREET,
LONDON, W.1.

Mr. Evan-Thomas

requests the honour of a visit from

. . . .

and Friends

to an

EXHIBITION

of Rare Examples of the
Art and Craft
of the
Wood-Turners
in the early 17th century

———

June 5th to June 30th

10.0 to 6.0   Sats., 10.0 to 1.0

P.T.O.

The Exhibits include

Twelve Armorial " Steeple-Cups "

and " Standing-Cups " dating from

1608 to 1620

*The largest and most important collection that has
ever been on view*

also

Early " Lamb's Wool " and " Wassail-Bowls,"

as well as Drinking cups of the 17th century,

many of them fine examples of the skill of the

Engine-Turners of this period

The proof of Evan-Thomas' invitation to the June 1939 exhibition.

Owen Evan-Thomas' press cutting book was obviously intended to be filled with reviews of his 1932 book entitled *Domestic Utensils of Wood*. In fact this contains no reviews but copies of photographs, some of which were used in the book but others that were not included. It also includes a loose leaf folder with some reviews and correspondence pertaining to his June 1939 exhibition. These are a unique record and seemed to be of sufficient historical and general interest to treen collectors to include extracts here.

Extracts from Evan-Thomas' press cuttings relating to his exhibition of 1939

Licensing World
8th July 1939

RARE CUPS

An exhibition of "steeple-cups" and "standing cups", rare wooden drinking vessels now worth £2,000 and used by Royalty and on Communion tables centuries ago, is being held in London. The cups are so rare that only thirty are still in existence. Eleven of the cups exhibited are dated from 1608 to 1620, and one other 1636. Five of the cups bear the Royal Arms of James I, and on six others are carved the armorial badges representing families that held the office of the Lord Chamberlain of the Household to every Sovereign from Henry VII to James I. "Lamb's wool" bowls, "wassail-bowls" – vessels made to hold hot spiced ales – and other wonderful examples of the art and craft of the wood-turners of the seventeenth and early eighteenth centuries are among the exhibits. As rare as any is the silver-mounted maplewood "Mazer Bowl" (dated 1614), one of the first wooden drinking vessels to be used.

It is on record that "Mazers" were used at "church ales" – festivals which were sometimes held in the church itself and at which beer given by the parishioners was sold for the benefit of church charities – and at processional times. Some of these bowls are now the priceless possessions of the Church and the Universities. A fine selection of "wassail-bowls" includes a seventeenth century type with three taps, and another capable of holding five gallons of ale!

Bournemouth Daily Echo
8th July 1939

KING JAMES'S WOODEN CUPS

Old Royal Drinking Vessels

on Exhibition

An exhibition of "steeple-cups" and "standing cups", rare wooden drinking vessels now worth £2,000 and used by Royalty and on Communion tables centuries ago, is being held until July 8th at the Dover-street W., premises of Mr. Owen Evan Thomas.

An exhibition of this type has never before been held in this country. The cups are so rare that only thirty are still in existence. Eleven of the cups exhibited are dated from 1608 to 1620, and one other 1636.

Mr. Evan Thomas thinks the cups are of ecclesiastical origin, but as they are made of sycamore wood, he doubts whether they could have been used as chalices, which were invariably of metal.

"I presume," he said in an interview, "that they were chiefly intended to be placed on the Communion tables in the private chapels of the nobility and important gentry as a symbol of the Holy Eucharist."

...

"LAMB'S WOOL" A DRINK.

...Another exhibit is a wooden "Mether" or "Maeddher", a standing cup of quadrangular shape with a handle on each side. This was dug up from a peat-bog in Donegal in a wonderful state of preservation. The cup was associated with the drinking of a kind of beer flavoured with honey.

The "lamb's wool" bowls on display got their name from the frothy appearance of the spiced ale caused by the beating up of eggs and other ingredients in the beer.

Star
1st July 1939

CUPS USED BY
KINGS ON
SHOW IN
LONDON

... Mr. Evan Thomas thinks the cups are of ecclesiastical origin...

WARNING
TO SINNERS

"I presume," he said in an interview, "that they were chiefly intended to be placed on the Communion tables in the private chapels of the nobility and important gentry as a symbol of the Holy Eucharist.

"The beautifully incised inscriptions on the cups show that they were intended to serve as a warning to unrepentant sinners."

Next and following pages. Signatures of some of the guests attending the exhibition. Note that Edward Pinto was an early visitor.

Later pages include the signatures of various notables and renowned collectors, including Mr.and Mrs. C.R. Asprey, Sir William Burrell, Mr. and Mrs F. Mallett, Mr. and Mrs. Bertie Stern, etc., representatives from *The Times, Apollo, The Daily Telegraph* and the Victoria and Albert Museum, and etc.

NAME	ADDRESS
Mon Carnegie	
M. C. Lane Roberts	
T. Livingstone Bailey (Apollo)	
Ingenett— (Times)	
Sydney Sherman	_13 St. James's Place S.W.1_
R. H. S. Watson	
W. Mai	
Kitty. Wallace	
Falconer L. Wallace	
Winnie Portarrington	
A. Curtis Sandwich	
W. A. Taggatt.	
Herbert Finn	
Winifred Hodgson	_Montreal_
Janet Krolik	_Montreal_
Edward. H. Pinto	_24 Hamilton Terrace St Johns Wood N.W.8._

W. A. Thorpe
8 ??? Irvine

Anthony F. Muntzer
George H. ???
I. Napier
A. J. W. ???

Francis ??? Mallett
M. G. Burton
J. Eckman Jr.
Mrs Francis Mallett
Mrs J. Shannon Munn
H. H. Brakspear
W. Crawford Snowden
Daily Telegraph
Evening News —
Mrs Bertie Stern
Bertie Stern

Passage Farm. Penn.
Victoria & Albert Museum
Hayle Holcombe??? S.W. 7.
25. Dover St. W.1
27 ??? S.W.1
71. Albert Hall mans.
S.W. 7.
???

168 ??? S.W.1.
72 Devonshire ??? W.
Longwood Combe Down.
Hyde Park Hotel
29? Elizabeth Street. S.W.1
15 Cavendish rd., Brondesbury
2 Park St. W.1
— do. —

W. Sutherland, Greendale, Maidenhead.

Eva Travers Lewis

John G H Budd.

Algernon Tudor-Craig

H Roland Smith

H. Pearson.

hr. Cayzer.

Editorial Services, Ltd.
Halifax House
Strand
WC 2.

W.E. Wendlyman

J. Walmsley,   Waddington   Yorks W.R.

H. Skene.   8 Lennox Gdns. S. W. 1.

F. Egerton   1. Trevor   Square   S.W. 1

Katharine Venables Llewelyn

Cara Venables.   32 Egerton Gardens

Cecil Millar.   Epsom.

J. Lewis Motson   Egarth Ruthin

D. Hobhouse.   c/o Barclays' Bank, Wimbledon Common.
                                                    S.W.19

E.G. Troyte Bullock   Zeals House Wilts
                Sole

        J. - . Willoughby
Antoinette Gerard - June 27th 1939 -
        Arthur Verney
Jobson Horne .   26th June 1939 .

        J.K. Bushell   27 June 1939 .

J. Hindes, 21, Thorpe Bay Gdns., Thorpe Bay, Essex.
    J.G. Walker.   Collingtree Rectory, Northampton .
        J. Faus   40 St James Place   S.W.1
    velyn Johnson   129. Wigmore Street. W.1

        G. Ankettell   25. Egerton Terrace
                                                    S.4

Mary VanDuun Rogers - 1914 La Salle Av Minneapolis Minn. USA
Charles Bolles Rogers-   "   "
E.B. Pinder Davis   Bath Club. Dover St.
W.E. Albert   Tyrells Wood Leatherhead .
J.G. Albert   "   "
W.H. Miller
Chas H Brewer   7 Wickmere Drive
                        Harrow Weald Mdx

Extracts from Evan-Thomas' file of correspondence relating to his exhibition of 1939

[Annotated in his hand]

Mention of <u>wooden cups</u> being used at the banquet following the coronation of Charles II
from an old book entitled "A chronicle of the Kings of England" by Sir Richard Baker KT – being a contemporary book of the time.

(<u>Extract</u>) "Following other incidents the second course was brought up by the Gentlemen Pensioners with the former solemnity and the last dish being carried Erasmus Smith Esqr. He having delivered the same to the table presented the king with <u>three maple cups </u>on the behalf of Robert Bernham Esqr. who was seized of the Manor of Nether-Belsingham in the County of Kent."

[Also annotated in his hand]

Early Methers
originated in Ireland

Mether:
or Maeddher.
The name serived from the old English "Meodie", medd or mead, the drink always associated with the Mether consisting of herbs, rosemary, hissop and thyme, boiled with honey – "Meddyglyn" – a drink made of mead and peculiar to Wales – derived from the words "Meddya" (beating) and Llyn (water).
The two specimens on exhibition are probably 15th century.

by courtesy Sir William Burrell
The very rare specimen, all cut from the solid, was dug up in a peat box in Donegal – hence its wonderful state of preservation.
The other one had lost its bottom, otherwise in its original state.

Mead, under the name of "Midee", Greek "Medos" – it is mentioned by Priscus as wine made from honey and drunk at the "Hunnish Court in AD 448.

The later form of methers is like a cup with one handle, cut from the solid. This form were imported into England by the Irish who came over to Cornwall to work in the tin mines, and they became very popular in England and much used in the Inns and Public Houses.
One early specimen from Ireland, with the handle cut from the solid, has a Gaelic inscription *"Cead mils ffaitte"* (ten thousand welcomes).

Copy of a letter from Algernon Tudor-Craig to Owen Evan-Thomas dated 28.3.1939 and written from 60, Great Queen Street, London W.C.2:

I believe that I have found a certain connection between your covered standing cups, as I think they must all have been connected in some way with the office of the Lord

Chamberlain of the Household. Five of the badges mentioned by you are undoubtedly connected with that office, but I cannot find out anything about the porcupine or the goose. [Handwritten margin query:"Is the porcupine by any chance a bristled boar?"] The others are as follows:

1.   Badges: 1. A goat statant sable.
                 2. A wyvern vert holding in the mouth a sinister hand gules (the 'grene dragon' of William Herbert, Earl of Pembroke, Chamberlain of South Wales 1461-69).

    Charles (Somerset), Earl of Worcester, Baron Herbert, K.G., natural son of Henry (Beaufort), Duke of Somerset by Joan Hill. He was cupbearer to the king 1486 and Lord Chamberlain of the Household to Henry VII 1508-9 and to Henry VIII 1509-26; died 15 April 1526.

2.   Badge: An elephant.
    William (Sandys), Lord Sandys of the Vine, K.G., Lord Chamberlain of the Household to Henry VIII 1530-35; Died 1542.

3.   Badge: A greyhound courant gules collared sable.
    John (Williams), Lord Williams of Thame, Lord Chamberlain of the Household to Philip, King Consort of Queen Mary 1553-7; died 14 October 1559.

4.   Badge: A swan. (from the [unreadable] Bohun & Mandeville families)
    Henry (Carey), Lord Hunsdon, K. G., Lord Chamberlain of the Household to Queen Elizabeth 1585-91; died 25 July 1596.

5.   Badge: An ostrich argent, beaked, Membered and vorant a horseshoe or.
    John (Digby), Earl of Bristol, Vice-Chamberlain of the Household to James I 1616-25; died 21 January 1652-3.

I hope that this is what you want, as I am convinced that the badges referred to are a distinct indication of the five chamberlains mentioned.

                    Yours sincerely,

                    Algernon Tudor-Craig

Note: The "White Hart Lodged' was originally the badge of the Fair Maid of Kent and was used both by Richard II & Edward IV also by the Lisle family, but the latter apparently had no connection with the office of Lord Chamberlain (p.39 of your book).

Evan-Thomas showed eleven cups at this 1939 exhibition. Five bore the arms of James I. Six had armorial badges. There is no record of the details of which cups bore which badges or dates.

These appendices are intended to be a helpful guide both to the novice collector and to the expert. They are neither comprehensive nor complete. In particular some of the references are incomplete, but despite this I am hopeful that enthusiasts will find some guidance to help them on their way and that they may be able to provide additional information to be included in the future.

APPENDIX II

Museums Displaying Treen

Birmingham
Birmingham Museum and Art Gallery. Pinto Collection, the largest collection of treen on show in this country. Extensive and wide ranging, first port of call for all collectors. Much unseen in reserve collection

Bolton
Hall-i'-th'- Wood Folk Museum. Good kitchen, wonderful candlestand, good cradles, unusual pipe stand. Well worth a visit to see what remains of collection.

Brecon
Brecknock Museum. Splendid display of love spoons – a must for love spoon enthusiasts.

Cardiff
St.Fagans, Welsh Folk Museum. National Museum of Wales. Extensive collections both on show and in the reserve, especially if wider social history and context are important. Love spoons in particular but essential for any collector.

Doncaster
City Museum. Remarkable early coffee grinder, good salts, unusual searce and clothes pegs! Gerald Shaw collection. Sadly most in reserve collection, but willingly shown with notice.

Dublin
National Museum of Ireland. Major collection of methers and lámhógs. Not yet seen. Collection moving.

Edinburgh
National Museums of Scotland. Reputed to be important but closed for rebuilding.

Glasgow
Burrell Collection, Pollok Country Park, Glasgow. Highly important treen, some of Evan-Thomas' best pieces. Essential to visit, beautiful museum, excellent restaurant.

Gloucester
Folk Museum., Domestic Life & Rural Crafts.

Hartlebury Castle
Hereford and Worcester County Museum. Remnants of Tickenhill Collection. Domestic and social life in 19th century and 20th century.

Haslemere
Haslemere Museum. Important collection of European and Scandinavian Folk Art. Not particularly strong on British treen.

Lewes
Anne of Cleves House Museum. Household equipment including plenty of treen.

London
British Museum. Mazers and a few other pieces displayed. Amazing treasures in reserve collection.
Victoria and Albert Museum. A few highly important pieces displayed and rose engine turned ivory. Phenomenal treasures in reserve collection. Roundels, armorial cups and many other rarities in abundance. Hopefully the Museum will be sufficiently pestered by collectors to mount a permanent exhibition.
Geffrye Museum. Very little treen but well laid out rooms. Worth a visit for social context.

Luton
Stockwood Craft Museum. Simple museum of rural life and crafts. Main museum has bobbins and hatting items in reserve collection.

Reading
Institute of Agricultural History and Museum of English Rural Life. Excellent but very general and treen not specifically highlighted. Important background information. Well worth a visit.

Ryedale
Ryedale Folk Museum. Small. Rural crafts, not specifically treen. Simple background information.

Scarborough
Rotunda. One lonely but superb pearwood cup. Worth a detour.

Taunton
Somerset County Museum at Taunton Castle. Whistling cup and many other pieces. Not yet visited but sounds good.

Whitby
Museum. Small collection, rather ordinary. Interesting spice pot.

York
York Castle Museum. Large collection knitting sheaths, many attributed to specific locality. Truncheons galore. Large reserve collection, very strong on methers.

Germany
Loschnermusuem, Bahnhofstrasse 20, 09544 Neuhausen. Not visited but reputed to have large collection of nut-crackers.

USA
American Nutcracker Museum, Leavenworth. WA 98826, USA. Not visited but reputed to have large collection.

Appendix III

Dealers with an interest in Treen

but not necessarily much stock

Benjamin, S. (Halcyon Days)
14 Brook Street, London W.1
Tel: 0171-629-8811

Day, Anne and Roger (Day Antiques)
5 New Church Street, Tetbury, Glos.
Tel: 01666-502413

de Courcy-Ireland, Polly
PO Box 29, Alresford, Hants. SO24 9WP

Drewett, Rosemary (Town & Country Antiques)
34 Market Street, Bradford on Avon, Wilts.
Tel: 01225-867877

Eldridge, Brian (Eldridge Antiques)
99 Farringdon Road, London EC1R 3BT
Tel: 0171-837-0379

Fenwick, George (Fenwick & Fenwick)
88 High Street, Broadway. Worcs.
Tel: 01386-853227

Few, Ted (Ted Few)
97 Drakefield Road, London SW17
Tel: 0181-767-2314

Foster, Stephen (Stephen Foster)
Little Heysham, Forge Road, Naphill, Bucks.
By appointment only. Tel: 01494-562024

Foster, Tony and Eleanor (A. & E. Foster)
Little Heysham, Forge Road, Naphill, Bucks.
By appointment only. Tel: 01494-562024

Fox, John (Fox House Antiques)
No.2, Park Street Antiques, Stow on the Wold, Glos.

Gulley, Bernard (Bernard Gulley Antiques)
Lancotbury Manor, Beds.
By appointment only. Tel: 01582-60643

Hawkins, John and Emma (Hawkins and Hawkins)
9 Atholl Crescent, Edinburgh, Scotland
Tel: 0831-093198

Hopwell, Paul (Paul Hopwell Antiques)
30 High Street, West Haddon, Northants.
Tel: 01788-510636

Howard, Bruce (B.I.Howard)
By appointment only. Tel: 01984-632271

Jenkins, Andrew (Avon Antiques)
25/27 Market Street, Bradford on Avon, Wilts.
Tel: 01225-862052

Levi, David (David Levi Antiques)
Stands 3 & 4, Lipka's Arcade, 282 Westbourne Grove, Portobello Market, London W.11
Tel: 0378-518094

Marchant, Annie (Wenderton Antiques)
Tel: 01227-720295

Newsum, Mark (Mark Newsum Antiques)
2 High Street, Winchcombe, Glos.
Tel: 01242-603446

Plumridge, Mr. and Mrs. (Woodstock Antiques)
Woodstock House, Winterhill Way, Guildford, Surrey
Tel: 01483-565634

Robinson, Danny and Mary (Key Antiques)
11 Horsefair, Chipping Norton, Oxon.
Tel: 01608-643777

Roofe, Mary (Mary Roofe Antiques)
1 Stonemasons Court, Parchment Street, Winchester, Hants.
Tel: 01962-840613

Seligman. Maja and David (M. & D. Seligman)
37 Kensington Church Street, London W8 4LL
Tel: 0171-937-0400

Wharton, Tim (Tim Wharton Antiques)
24, High Street, Redbourne, Nr. St. Albans. Herts.
Tel: 01582-794371

Young, Robert (Robert Young Antiques)
68 Battersea Bridge Road, London SW11 3AG
Tel: 0171-228-7847

Books on Treen and Related Subjects

E.H. Pinto, *Treen and other Wooden Bygones,* 1969, Bell & Hyman, 0 7135 1533 3. Largest and most comprehensive book on treen – 'The Bible'.

E.H. Pinto, *Treen or Small Woodware Throughout the Ages,* 1949, B.T Batsford. Forerunner of 'The Bible'.

E.H. Pinto, *Wooden Bygones of Smoking and Snuff Taking,* 1961, Hutchinson & Co. Small specialist area covered more fully than in 'The Bible'.

E.H.Pinto, *The Craftsman in Wood,* 1962, G. Bell & Sons. Story of wood uses over ages with treen being prominent.

Owen Evan-Thomas, *Domestic Utensils of Wood,* 1932, EP Publishing, 0 85409 891 7. Record of major collector, dealer and expert.

S.G. Abell, J. Leggat and W.G. Ogden, Jr., *A Bibliography of The Art of Turning and Lathe and Machine Tool History,* 1950, Museum of Ornamental Turning.

N.W. Alcock & Linda Hal, *Fixtures and Fittings in dated Houses 1567-1763,* 1994, Council for British Archaeology, 1 872414 52 4.

Paul Anex et al., *Arts et Metiers du Vin,* 1994, Cabedita, 2 88295 123 X.

C. Arminjon and N. Blondel, *Objets Civil Domestiques,* 1984, Imprimerie Nationale, 2 11 080812 8.

Douglas Ash, *English Silver Drinking Vessels 600-1830,* 1964, G. Bell and Sons.

Brian Austen, *Tunbridge Ware,* 1989, W. Foulsham and Co., 0 572 01466 X.

L.E. Bergeron, *Manuel du Tourneur,* 1792, Paris.

Peter Brears, *The Kitchen Catalogue,* Castle Museum, York, 1979.

Fred. W. Burgess, *Chats on Household Curios,* 1914, T. Fisher Unwin.

John Caspall, *Making Fire and Light,* 1987, Antique Collectors' Club, 1 85149 021 3.

Victor Chinnery, *Oak Furniture,* 1979, Antique Collectors' Club, 0 902028 61 8.

Professor A.H. Church, *Some Minor Arts,* 1894, Seeley & Co. Chapter on Old English Fruit Trenchers, pp.47-54.

Erland Fenn Clark, *Truncheons,* 1935, Herbert Jenkins Ltd.

A.J. Conybeare, *Trees Chests and Boxes,* 1991, Self Pub.Association, 1 85421 142 0. Masterly pair of books. Dendrochronology, style and dating.

A.J. Conybeare, *A Discourse on Boxes,* 1992, ROSCA Pubs., 0 9517678 1 X. All covered well. Outstanding.

W.J. Cripps, *Old English Plate,* 1901, reprinted, 1977, EP Publishing, 0 7158 1236.

Tony Curtis, *Town and Country Kitchens,* 1992, Bracken Books, 1 95170 913 4.

Pierre Delacretaz, *Les vieux fours à pain,* 1993, Cabedita, 2 88295 089 6.

Caroline Earwood, *Domestic Wooden Artefacts,* 1993, University of Exeter Press, 0 85989 389 8.

Bernard Estridge, *A Catalogue of Irish Methers,* 1983, Queen's University, Belfast.

J.E. Evans, *Ornamental Turning,* 1886, London.

Helen E. FitzRandolph and M. Doriel Hay, *The Rural Industries of England and Wales,* 1977, EP Publishing. Chapter on Timber and Underwood Industries etc.

Anne Forty, *Treen and Earthenware,* 1979, Midas Books, 0 85936 074 1. Unambitious. Very simple.

Linda Campbell Franklin, *300 years of Kitchen Collectibles,* 1984, Books Americana, 0 89689 041 4.

R. Gentle and Rachel Feild, *Domestic Metalwork 1640-1820,* 1994, Antique Collectors' Club, 1 85149 187 2.

Christopher Gilbert, *English Vernacular Furniture, 1750-1900,* 1991, Yale University Press, 0 300 04762 2.

Mary Earle Gould, *Early American Wooden Ware,* 1962, Charles E. Tuttle, 0 8048 0153 3.

Jean Guibal, *Les Objets de la Vie Quotidienne dans Les Alpes,* 1990, Glenat, 2 7234 1297 0.

Bertrand B. Guilian, *Corkscrews of the Eighteenth Century,* 1995, White Space Publishers.

Bente Gundestup, *The Royal Danish Kunstkammer, 1737,* 1995, Copenhagen National Museum.

H.L. Harlan and W.C. Anderson, *Duck Calls,* 1988, Harlan-Anderson.

Arthur Hayden, *Chats on Old Silver,* 1952, Ernest Benn.

Peter Hornsby, *Collecting Antique Copper and Brass,* 1989, Moorland Publishing, 0 86190 118 5.

Holtzapffel, *Turning Mechanical and Manipulation.*

Bernard and Therle Hughes, *Three Centuries of English Domestic Silver,* 1952, Lutterworth Press.

Charles James Jackson, *History of English Plate,* 1911, B.T. Batsford.

J. Geraint Jenkins, *Bowl Turners and Spoon Carvers,* Folk Art.

Allan Jobson, *Household and Country Crafts,* 1953, Elek.

Mary Eirwen Jones, *Welsh Crafts,* 1978, B.T.Batsford, 0 7134 1087 6.

Paul E. Kindig, *Butter Prints and Molds,* 1986, Schiffer, 0 88740 058 2.

Claudia Kinmonth, *Irish Country Furniture 1700-1950,* 1993, Yale University Press, 0 300 05574 9. Chapter on Methers and Lámhógs, pp.195-202.

David Knell, *English Country Furniture,* 1992, Barrie & Jenkins, 0 7126 3943-8.

J. Seymour Lindsay, *Iron and Brass Implements of the English House,* 1964, Alec Tiranti.

Carl F. Luckey, *Collecting Antique Bird Decoys and Duck Calls,* 1992, Books Americana.

James Lukin, *The Lathe and its Uses,* 1868, Trubner, London.

Arthur Macgregor, *Tradescant's Rarities, Essays on the Foundations of the Ashmolean Museum 1683.*

Wolf Mankowitz, *Make Me an Offer,* 1952, André Deutsch.

Martin Mathews, *Engine Turning 1680-1980.*

Maurice, *Sovereigns as Turners,* 1985.

Mervyn Mitton, *The Policeman's Lot,* 1985, Quiller Press, 0 907621 50 3.

G.J. Monson-Fitzjohn, *Drinking Vessels of Bygone Days,* 1927, Herbert Jenkins. Fascinating old book. Not comprehensive.

J. Moxon, *Mechanical Exercises of the Doctrine of Handy Works,* 1975, reprint of 1703 edition.

Reginald Myer, *Chats on Old English Tobacco Jars,* Sampson Low, Marston. Records and comment on very major old collection.

George Nicolle, *The Woodworking Trades,* 1993, Twybill Press, 0 9522285 0 5.

Mary Norwak, *Kitchen Antiques,* 1975, Praeger, 0 275 22040-0.

Ogden, *The Pedigree of the Holtzapffel Lathe,* 1987.

Trefor M. Owen, *Welsh Folk Customs,* 1968.

I Peate ed., *Studies in Regional Consciousness and Environment,* 1930, Oxford University Press. Chapter 12, Some Welsh Wood-Turners and their Trade, Iorwerth Peate.

E.H. & E.R. Pinto, *Tunbridge & Scottish Souvenir Woodware,* 1970, G. Bell & Sons, 0 7135 1772 7.

C. Plumier, *The Art of Turning,* 1975, translation of French 1749 edition.

T.R. Poole, *Identifying Antique British Silver,* 1988, Bloomsbury, 0 7475 0092-4.

Gherardo Priuli, *I Legni Antichi Della Montagna,* 1988, Collana: I Grandi Libri.

C. Proudfoot and P. Walker, *Woodworking Tools,* 1984, Phaidon-Christie's, 0 7148 8005 1.

M. Redknap ed., *Artefacts from Wrecks,* 1997, Oxbow Books, 1 900188 39 2. Chapter 4. The Material Culture of the Mary Rose, Alex Hildred.

Judith A. Rittenhouse, *Ornamental and Figural Nutcrackers,* Collector Books, USA.

Walter Rose, *The Village Carpenter,* 1937, Stobart Davies, 0 85442 065 7.

Alistair Sampson, *Cabinet Secrets,* 1987, Robson Books, 0 86051 452 8.

P. de Santis and M. Fantoni, *The Corkscrew,* 1990, Marzorati Editore, 88 280 0098 8.

P.N. and H. Schiffer, *The Brass Book,* 1978, Schiffer, 0 916838 17 X.

John Seymour, *Forgotten Household Crafts,* 1987, Dorling Kindersley, 0 86318 174 0.

Suzanne Slesin et al., *Garden Tools,* 1996, Abbeville Press, 0 7892 0087 2.

Jeffrey B. Snyder, *Canes,* 1993, Schiffer, 0 88740 549 5.

Jeanne et Michel Sonkin, *L'Objet Paysan,* Ch. Masan.

David Starkey, ed., *Henry VIII, A European Court in England.*

Francis W. Steer, *Farm and Cottage Inventories of Mid-Essex,* 1635-1749, 1969, Phillimore.

Roy Strong, *The English Renaissance Miniature,* Yale University Press.

Jane Toller, *Turned Woodware for Collectors,* 1975, A.S. Barnes & Co., 0 498 01830 X. Chatty informative book.

Jane Toller, *Searching for Antiques,* 1970, Ward Lock.

Jane Toller, *Country Furniture,* 1973, David and Charles, 0 7153 6029 9.

Jane Toller, *Living with Antiques,* 1968, Ward Lock.

B.M. Watney and H.D. Babbage, *Corkscrews for Collectors,* 1993, Sotheby's Publications, 0 85667 431 1.

P. Weiner and C. Kiado. *Carved Honeycake Moulds,* 1964, 963-13-0893-6.

George Whiteman, *The Collector's Round,* 1971, G. Bell & Sons, 0 7135 1673 9.

Anne Mortimer Young, *Antique Medicine Chests,* 1995, Vernier Press, 1 898825 02 5.

Articles on Treen and Related Subjects

Richard Ballam, 'Solitaire and Other Turned Boards', *Antique Collecting,* October 1992, Vol. 27, No. 5, pp.48-51.

Peter C.D. Brears, 'The Knitting Sheath', *Folk Life,* 1981, Vol. 20, pp.16-40.

H. Clifford Smith, 'Heraldic Wooden Cups of the Jacobean Period, The Property of Sir Gerald Ryan, Bart', *Connoisseur,* 1924, LXVIII, 269.3-10.

J. Ferguson and R. Davies, 'A Survey of Tudor and Early Jacobean Rose Turning', *Bulletin* No. 83, The Society of Ornamental Turners.

Richard Filmer, 'Pole Lathes and the Chiltern Chair Bodger', Part 1, *Period Home,* Vol. 6, No. 5, pp.31-34.

Richard Filmer, 'Pole Lathes. The Ancient Craft of Bowl Turning', Part 2, *Period Home,* Vol. 6, No. 6, pp.25-27.

W.H. St.John Hope, 'On the English medieval drinking bowls called Mazers', *Archeologica,* 1887, Vol. L, pp.129-194.

Peter Hornsby, 'Wooden Plates', *Antique Collecting,* September 1992, Vol. 27, No. 4, pp.19-24.

G.E.P. How, 'Scottish Standing Mazers', *Proceedings of the Society of Antiquities of Scotland,* 1933, Vol. 68, pp.394-411.

W.T. O'Dea, 'Making Fire', H.M. Stationery Office, 1964.

Edward H .Pinto, 'Treen Cups for an Exclusive Society' *Country Life,* 30 March 1967.

E.H. Pinto, 'Hand-made Combs', *Connoisseur,* p.170.

Richard A. Price, 'Ship Timber Souvenirs', *Antique Collecting,* September 1996, Vol. 31, No. 4, pp. 38-40.

J.Y. Akerman, 'An Account of some "Roundells" or Fruit Trenchers etc.', *Archaeologia,* 1851, Vol. 34, pp.225-230.

Charles R. Beard, 'Wedding Knives', *Connoisseur,* February 1930, pp.91-97.

Cyril Bunt, 'Wooden Domestic Utensils of Treen', *Antique Dealer & Collectors Guide,* May 1960, pp.36-37.

W. Ruskin Butterfield, 'About Knitting Sheaths', *Connoisseur,* January 1919, pp.18-24.

Victor Chinnery, 'Early Oak Furniture', *Antique Collecting,* July/August 1993, Vol. 28, No. 3, pp.14-15.

Brent Elliott, 'A History of Tools', *The Garden,* January 1995, pp.40-43.

David J. Eveleigh, 'Victorian Kitchen Gadgets', *Antique Collecting,* September 1993, Vol. 28, No. 4, pp.22-25.

Sally Kevill-Davies, 'Elizabethan Fruit Trenchers', *Antique Collecting,* December 1987, Vol. 22, No. 7, p.56.

A.P.L., 'A Wooden Box for Christmas', *Antique Collecting,* November 1980, Vol. 15, No. 6, p.18.

Kate Mason, 'Yorkshire Cheese Making', *Folk Life,* 1967, 6, pp.7-17.

'Old English Fruit Trenchers', *Portfolio,* 1885, 9 and 10.

Evan Owen-Thomas, Catalogue from Exhibition of Early Wooden Drinking Cups, 23 May to 21 June 1921.

Barbara Pearce, ' a Cubbord with a Treen vessell...', *Antique Collecting,* April 1985, Vol. 19, No. 11, pp.40-44.

E.H. Pinto, 'Mazers and their Wood', *Connoisseur,* 1949, pp.33-36.

Edward.H .Pinto, 'Pictures written in fire', *Country Life,* 20 April 1961.

Edward.H .Pinto, 'Wooden Mortars and Grinders' *Antiques Review,* pp.21-24.

Fred Roe, 'The Art of the Cofferer', *Connoisseur,* March 1916, Vol. 44, p.123.

Fred Roe, 'Bible Boxes', *Connoisseur,* December 1930, pp.377-383.

Fred Roe, 'Old Furniture', *Connoisseur,* pp.199-208.

Sheelah Ruggles-Brise, 'Some "Royal" Coffers', *Connoisseur,* August 1952, pp.19-23.

Alison Scott, 'Treen', *Antique Collecting,* November 1987, Vol. 22, No. 6, pp.14-17.

Mark Stephen, 'A Gift of Treen', *Antique Collecting,* December 1989, Vol. 24, No. 7, p.19.

Mark Stephen, 'Collecting Treen', *Antique Collecting,* September 1990, Vol. 25, No. 4, pp. 24-26.

R.W. Symonds, 'The Regional Design and Ornament of Joined Furniture', *Connoisseur,* June 1948, pp.90-96.

Jane Toller, 'Treen Candlesticks', *Antique Collecting,* January 1973, Vol. 7, No. 9, pp.7-9

Jane Toller, 'Treen Drinking Cups', *Antique Collecting,* February 1972, Vol. 7, No. 10, pp.8-11.

Jane Toller, 'Treen Spoons and Ladles', *Antique Collecting,* March 1972, Vol. 7, No. 11, pp.5-7.

Jane Toller, 'Buying and Collecting Treen', *Antique Collecting,* January 1974, Vol. 8, No. 9, pp.44-46..

Julia W. Torrey, 'Some Early Variants of the Windsor Chair', *Antiques,* September 1922, pp.106-110.

W.W.Watts, 'Old English "Treen Ware"', *Apollo,* June 1939, pp.290-292.

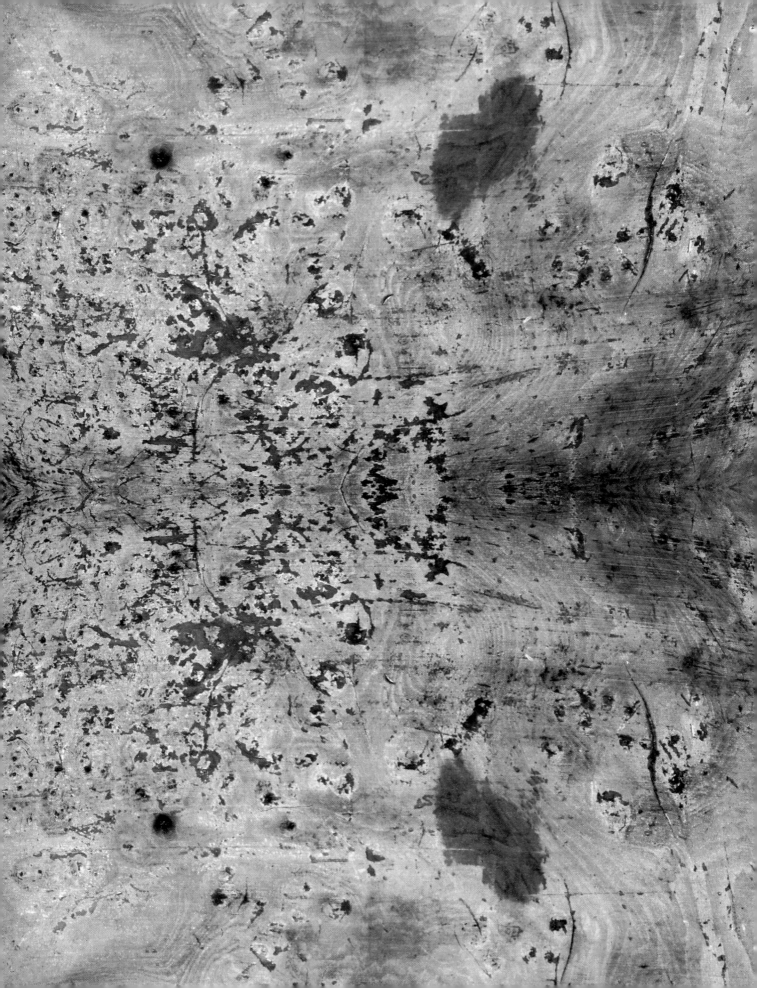